A HISTORY OF THE SECOND BATTALION
THE MONMOUTHSHIRE REGIMENT.

GWELL ANGAU NA GWARTH.

South Africa, 1900-02.

"**Ypres, 1915,** '17, '18," "Gravenstafel," "**St. Julien,**" "Frezenberg," "Bellewaarde," "**Somme, 1916,**" "Albert, 1916," "**Arras, 1917,**" "**Scarpe, 1917,**" "Pilckem," "**Langemarck, 1917,**" "Poelcappelle," "**Cambrai, 1917,** '18," "Lys," "Messines, 1918," "**Hindenburg Line,**" "St. Quentin Canal," "Beaurevoir," "Courtrai," "Sambre," "**France and Flanders, 1914,** '18," "Aden."

LIEUT.-COLONEL A. J. H. BOWEN, D.S.O.
Commanding Officer 1915 - 1917
Killed in Action March 2nd, 1917.

A HISTORY

OF

The 2nd Battalion
The Monmouthshire Regiment

COMPILED BY

CAPTAIN G. A. BRETT, D.S.O., M.C.
The South Wales Borderers
(24th Regiment).

PONTYPOOL:
HUGHES AND SON, THE GRIFFIN PRESS.
1933.

FOREWORD.

When preparing this record of the 2nd Battalion The Monmouthshire Regiment, my task was greatly facilitated by the ease of access to documents which my appointment as Adjutant to the Battalion afforded. There were many old papers of early days, amid which Colonel Mitchell's " History of the Volunteer Movement in Monmouthshire " (published in 1908) was of real assistance in shedding light on otherwise obscure points. The second and third chapters rest mainly upon the admirable summaries contained in Colonel Sir Joseph Bradney's Annual Circular Letters to all ranks, while the South African War period is compiled partly from these letters and other papers, and partly from a history of the services of the 2nd Battalion The South Wales Borderers in that campaign.

The War Diary for 1914-1918 was made out apparently in triplicate. The original is in the possession of the Historical Section of the Committee for Imperial Defence, and was not, I thought, necessary for the purposes of this record. The duplicate, lost portions of which were made up from the third copy, has now totally disappeared. The remainder of the third copy, covering from March, 1916, to May, 1917, and from April, 1918, to May, 1919, was in Colonel Evans' possession, and he placed it, together with copies of the 29th and 34th Divisional Histories, at my disposal. The other portions of the war periods have been carefully checked with the Official History of the War and the " Story of the 29th Division," and I have perused all Battalion Routine Orders published in the field from the beginning of 1916 onwards. In addition, I came across an excellent diary of the winter 1916-17 written by Major H. W. E. Bailey.

A battalion was a very small unit in a war such as that which raged from 1914 to 1918, and beyond now and then describing events sufficiently to "paint the picture," I have avoided, I trust, writing anything approaching a history of the war or any action in it. I have relied for narrations of episodes on participants in them, to the appeal for which the response was wide. It may be invidious to mention some names where so many helped, but Major T. L. Ibbs and Captains C. Comely and E. G. Foster have gone to considerable trouble in amplifying and correcting the narrative, while Captain R. T. Saunders supplied information on the duties and methods of a Pioneer Battalion which will not readily be found elsewhere, and Lieutenant J. A. Burgoyne has lent some interesting photographs. Some contributions have been repeated verbatim, some have been altered or reduced, and many have unfortunately been omitted. I am very grateful to those of all ranks who sent them, for even anecdotes which have been omitted have helped to re-create the atmosphere.

To Lieutenant H. Ll. Hughes is owing a deep debt of gratitude from his old Regiment. Not only has he thrown himself whole-heartedly into the task of obtaining material, but his help in arranging the matter for publication has enabled the firm of which he is head to produce the book at so low a price.

This attempt to place on paper a record of the Battalion has been to me a source of pleasure, and I hope the 2nd Mons. will accept it as a memento of my four happy years with them.

G.A.B.

CONTENTS.

CHAPTER		PAGE
	Introduction	11
I.	2nd Monmouthshire Rifle Volunteer Corps, 1858–85	13
II.	3rd Volunteer Bn. South Wales Borderers, 1885–1908	19
III.	2nd Bn. Monmouthshire Regiment, T.F., 1908–1914	28
IV.	1/2nd Battalion Monmouthshire Regiment .. The First Winter in Flanders—Mining—" Ypres, 1915 " — The Amalgamated Regiment — The Somme in 1915—On the Lines of Communication	34
V.	Conversion to Pioneers—Return to the Somme—" Somme, 1916 "—Interlude at Ypres—Back to the Somme—Le Transloy—Sailly-Saillisel ..	50
VI.	" Scarpe, 1917 "—" Ypres, 1917 "—" Pilckem " — " Langemarck, 1917 " — " Poelcapelle " — " Cambrai, 1917 "	75
VII.	Ypres Salient—The Battle of the Lys	91
VIII.	The Turning of the Tide—Outtersteene—Steenwercke—" Ypres, 1918 "—" Messines, 1918 "—" Courtrai "—The Armistice—March into Germany—Pontypool Once More	103
IX.	The 2/2nd and 3/2nd Battalions—The Depot—1st Volunteer Bn. The Monmouthshire Regiment	115
X.	2nd Bn. Monmouthshire Regiment, T.A., 1920–1932	122

APPENDICES.

A.	Rules of 2nd Monmouthshire Rifle Volunteers, 1860	125
B.	Rules of 3rd V.B. South Wales Borderers, 1891 ..	130
C.	Notes on Stations and Companies	135
D.	Rolls of Officers	140
E.	Honorary Colonels, Commanding Officers & Adjutants	146
F.	List of Annual Camps	147
G.	Honours and Awards, 1914 – 1918	148
H.	Roll of Honour, 1914 – 1918	151

ILLUSTRATIONS

FACING PAGE

Portrait of Lieut.-Colonel A. J. H. Bowen, D.S.O. (Killed in Action).	*Frontispiece*
Portrait of Colonel R. B. Roden	17
Portrait of Colonel T. Mitchell	20
Portrait of Colonel Sir Joseph Bradney, C.B., T.D.	29
Portrait of Brigadier-General E. B. Cuthbertson, C.M.G., M.V.O.	32
Photographs in the Ypres Salient, 1915	40, 41
Portrait of Colonel John Evans, D.S.O., T.D.	74
The Colours in Germany The Return to Pontypool	113
Portrait of Colonel W. R. Lewis, T.D.	123
The Officers, Aberystwyth Camp, 1931	124

MAPS

2nd Battle of Ypres	44
Battle of Cambrai, 1917	88
Battle of the Lys	103
Key map shewing movements of the Battalion in France, 1914-1918	112

INTRODUCTION

by General Sir Beavoir de Lisle, K.C.B., K.C.M.G., D.S.O.

THE distinguished record of the achievements of the 2nd Battalion, The Monmouthshire Regiment is one that must fill everyone who is in any way connected with this splendid corps with the utmost pride.

The History prepared by Captain Brett, D.S.O., M.C., is intensely interesting, with just sufficient detail to maintain the interest without giving too much prominence to individual action.

When this Regiment joined the 29th Division in 1916 as the Pioneer Battalion its fine fighting record with the 4th Division since November, 1914, was well known and the whole Division soon recognised its good fortune in the addition of a fighting unit whose discipline and sense of duty compared favorably with the other distinguished units which composed the 29th.

Many of the best achievements of the 29th Division in France and Belgium were indirectly due to the work of this Regiment—one of the most notable instances was the reconstruction of the defences in the Ypres Salient in 1916, a task which had defeated many distinguished Divisions. This difficult work was carried out so satisfactorily that the Corps Commander was enabled to conduct His Majesty, the King of the Belgians, round the front line trenches without his boots being soiled, and a special order thanking the 29th was issued by General Sir Herbert Plumer, the Commander of the 2nd Army.

Early in 1917 on the Somme front both at Le Transloy and at Sailly-Saillisel the work of the Divisional Pioneers was most remarkable and enabled the areas won to be successfully held in spite of several heavy counter attacks. On both these occasions the congratulations received from higher Commanders were most complimentary to the Division and to the Monmouthshire Regiment.

On the latter occasion the elation of all units of the 29th, customary after every marked success, was marred by the loss of that distinguished leader, Lieut.-Colonel A. J. H. Bowen, D.S.O., an officer who always displayed so high a standard of efficiency and sense of duty.

The difficult and dangerous work of the Pioneer Battalion of a fighting Division is well brought out in their History but with no suspicion of exaggeration. Working principally at night in shell swept areas, often unprotected by any defences, the Pioneers are exposed to a greater nerve strain than any other unit, a strain that can only be endured by men physically fit who have been imbued with a high sense of discipline and whose leaders can always be trusted to set an example of courage and determination to complete a duty, however difficult and however dangerous.

BEAUVOIR DE LISLE,
General
(late Commanding 29th Division).

Devizes,
24 February, 1933.

CHAPTER I.

2ND MONMOUTHSHIRE RIFLE VOLUNTEER CORPS 1858 – 1885.

VOLUNTEER units had been in existence during the Napoleonic struggles, but in the peaceful years which followed Waterloo they were disbanded, and the national defences entrusted entirely to the regular forces. Immersed in vast new industrial developments, the nation for many years took little interest in martial affairs. The horrors of the Indian Mutiny, however, followed by the strain of the Crimean War, stirred the dormant fighting instincts of its men, and when a long French campaign of antagonism culminated in 1859 in a violent and insulting outburst in the Parisian newspapers, the nation, stung to the quick, literally sprang to arms, volunteer corps coming spontaneously into existence all over the country.

Slow to action at first, the Government decided eventually to sanction the movement. They issued a Circular in May, 1859, to the Lord Lieutenants inaugurating the Volunteer Force and authorising the enrolment of Volunteers in Artillery and Rifle Corps. So great was the enthusiasm that in less than a year nearly 120,000 men had enrolled for service.

A later Circular stated that no cost whatever would be borne by the public, and that no pecuniary assistance would be given. Volunteers in consequence had to provide their own uniforms and accoutrements, and in many instances even their own rifles. In the beginning money poured in : sums were voted by municipal bodies, private donors gave munificently, and concerts and bazaars for raising funds were enthusiastically patronized. But as the apprehension of invasion died down, increasing difficulty was found in maintaining units, for armouries, drill halls and rifle ranges had to be kept up and instructors, generally old soldiers, had to be paid.

2ND MONMOUTHSHIRE RIFLE VOLUNTEER CORPS

The Government's first concession was the provision of 25 per cent. of the rifles, later increased to the full number on the enrolled strength. Next they provided adjutants and drill instructors from the Regular Army. It was evident, however, as early as 1862 that the Volunteer Force would soon disappear unless it received aid from public funds, and Parliament, after hearing the report of a Royal Commission of that year, authorized the payment of a Capitation Grant to commanding officers for the maintenance and administration of their units.

This Grant was based at first at the rate of 30s. for each efficient volunteer; later it was increased to 35s., and in the cases of officers and sergeants to 50s. It enabled units to be independent of outside help, and while certain other financial concessions were given subsequently, it remained the principal source of income during the life of the Volunteer Force. Through it, uniforms and equipment were purchased for the men, and drill halls and ranges provided for the companies. To qualify as "efficient" and earn the grant for his corps, a Volunteer had to perform nine drills in the year (thirty if a recruit), fire a musketry course, and be present at the annual inspection parade.

In Monmouthshire the Volunteer movement began with the formation of Corps (or companies of 100 men) in the various towns, precedence within the county being taken in accordance with the date of formation. Chepstow and Pontypool had the honour of raising the first two corps, and a dispute as to their relative precedence, which arose after the official recognition of the Volunteer Force, was determined by the fact that Chepstow had preceded Pontypool by one day in rendering names to the Lord Lieutenant. The latter Corps, therefore, which had been raised by Mr. R. B. Roden, in December, 1858, became the 2nd Monmouthshire Rifle Volunteer Corps.

Early in 1859, a Corps was raised in Abersychan, and in May Corps were formed in Abercarn and Sirhowy, while two were enrolled at Ebbw Vale. These five Corps were consolidated with that at Pontypool into a battalion, which took the name of its senior company, and Captain Roden was gazetted to the command with the rank of Lieutenant-Colonel on 8th December, 1860. Headquarter offices were established at Bank Chambers, Pontypool, where the Post Office now stands, and in the following May Captain J. O. Carnegie, 21st Regiment, joined as adjutant. About the same period four regular sergeants were posted as drill instructors.

Thus the seed of the present battalion was sown, but a slight digression into the history of other units is necessary to show the root-source of certain branches which came to be grafted on to the battalion tree when in the course of time some sturdy limbs had to be lopped off.

The other Corps (or companies) in the county retained their identities as separate units, even for a time to the extent of wearing different uniforms. They were, however, grouped into two battalions, the 1st and 2nd Administrative Battalions Monmouthshire Rifle Volunteers, although they only came under the control of their commanding officers on the rare occasions of battalion parades. The 2nd Administrative Battalion had its headquarters also at Pontypool, where it had raised the "Hanbury" Corps in November, 1859. This unit, now the 3rd Battalion Monmouthshire Regiment, had raised in 1859 and 1860 other Corps at Blaenavon, Monmouth and Usk, all of which are now stations of the 2nd Monmouthshire Regiment. It shared, therefore, in the parentage of this Battalion, and it will be shown later how the 2nd (Consolidated) Battalion in return contributed to the present 3rd Monmouthshires.

Rules* for the 2nd Monmouthshire Rifle Volunteers were agreed to and passed at a General Meeting of the Corps, held at Pontypool on 5th January, 1860. The appointment under these Rules of a Committee of all ranks, "to aid the Commanding Officer in the non-military affairs of the Corps," exemplifies the civilian character of the organization. Among other subjects dealt with in the Rules, perhaps the most interesting are those governing entry into the Corps, the rates of subscription, and the scale of fines for infractions of discipline.

No regulation pattern uniform was laid down by the War Office, and Corps were free to choose their own: hence the bright array of Yeomanry and Volunteer uniforms which dazzled the public eye about 1860. The 2nd Monmouthshires selected a sober grey, "pepper and salt," with a shako of the same colour

* See Appendix A.

ornamented with a green ball for full dress. In undress uniform they wore a " kepi." The band at this period had white jackets trimmed with blue. In 1864, in common with other Volunteers of the county, the Battalion adopted Rifle Brigade dress of dark green, with black belts and shakos. In the following year the Corps departed from the county dress by changing the black facings for the brighter red of the 60th Rifles. The shako was retained, though with obvious reluctance, for " Bersaglieri " hats presented by Lady Llanover were tried out for a season on the Abersychan company, and a year or so afterwards the smart busby of the 60th Rifles was adopted. In 1874, the 2nd Battalion led the way in Monmouthshire in following line regiments rather than rifle by changing to scarlet tunics, with green facings. The busby, however, was retained until 1878, when it was replaced by the regulation helmet.

In 1861, Colours made by Mrs. Hanbury Leigh and ladies of the county were presented to the Battalion.

The first parade of the Battalion was on the occasion of a review of Monmouthshire Volunteers in Pontypool Park, on Whit-Monday, 1861, when Mrs. Hanbury Leigh presented on behalf of her husband, then Lord Lieutenant, a silver bugle to each Commanding Officer. The earliest parade state now available shows 17 Officers, 24 Sergeants and 325 Rank and File present at Ebbw Vale on the 1st March, 1863, and is of special interest in that this parade was in honour of the marriage of T.R.H. The PRINCE OF WALES and PRINCESS ALEXANDRA OF DENMARK.

The annual inspection parade was the most important function, militarily and socially, of the year, and to it were invited the relatives and friends of all members of the Corps. It was held at different towns each year until 1879, after which advantage was taken of the Battalion being in camp. The inspection usually included battalion drill under the Commanding Officer, following which other officers would be directed to put the battalion through the " manual exercises " and " platoon drill."

The first encampment of Monmouthshire Volunteers took place in 1880 when the 2nd Battalion camped for a week at Llanthewy Skirrid, near Abergavenny. This was the beginning

Colonel R. B. RODEN
Commanding Officer 1859 - 1887.

2ND MONMOUTHSHIRE RIFLE VOLUNTEER CORPS

of the most popular feature in regimental life, appreciated as much to-day by the Territorials as by their Volunteer ancestors. During the lifetime of the Volunteer Force, the annual camp lasted for one week only. A great deal of ceremonial drill was performed, and field days were held in which tactical evolutions were practised. On inspection days the officers gave a lunch to which regimental guests and personal friends were invited, battalion sports being held in the afternoon.

The primary object of Rifle Corps was to further a sound knowledge of musketry, and indeed the War Office directed soon after the Volunteer Force had been inaugurated that " rifle practice rather than complicated drill " was to be pursued. The 2nd Monmouthshires took an active interest in shooting, held frequent meetings, and participated in all county rifle competitions, being particularly encouraged by Colonel Roden who, owning the patent of the Snider rifle, had special technical interests and qualifications. The earliest notable success was in 1864 when Private George Joshua carried off the Lord Lieutenant's medal at a county meeting at Newport.

Between its formation in 1858 and its change of name in 1885 the Battalion led the busy and useful but uneventful life common to all Volunteer units. It met other units at field days and reviews, acquired an excellent reputation, and laid the foundation of a sound *esprit de corps*. Much the most notable event in this period was the Grand Volunteer Review at Windsor in 1881 before Her Majesty QUEEN VICTORIA, at which the Battalion, 400 strong, with two companies attached from the 1st Battalion, represented the County.

GWELL ANGAU NA GWARTH.

Regimental mottoes are rare in the British Army, and now that the Brecknockshire Battalion S.W.B. has ceased to exist as a separate entity, the 2nd Monmouthshires are unique among Welsh and Welsh Border Battalions in possessing one.

Its origin dates back to the period when Sir Benjamin Hall, afterwards Lord Llanover, became Lord Lieutenant of the County about 1864. His wife was an enthusiast on the Volun-

2ND MONMOUTHSHIRE RIFLE VOLUNTEER CORPS

teer movement, and it is related that at one review " she mounted a horse and galloped round, doing more than all the work of an inspecting officer." Although not a Welshwoman by birth, she took the deepest interest in Welsh affairs, becoming a great patron of Modern Welsh. She composed the motto (in English, " Rather Death Than Dishonour "), and persuaded her husband to force it on the County Volunteers against the opposition of those who held that Monmouthshire was not a Welsh county. Only the 2nd Battalion still retains it.

The first officers and their company stations on the formation of the Battalion were as follows :—

Headquarters, Pontypool. Lt.-Col. R. B. Roden, Commanding.
Adjutant : Captain J. O. Carnegie, late 21st Foot.
Surgeons : James Essex, E. E. Tucker.
Chaplain : Rev. W. Hughes, M.A.

Company.		Captains.	Lieutenants.	Ensigns.
No. I.	Pontypool	W. B. Hawkins	—	A. Edwards
,, II.	Ebbw Vale	W. Adams	—	—
,, III.	Abersychan	J. Richards	E. Tothill	T. Mitchell
,, IV.	Ebbw Vale	H. Laxton	J. Browne	P. James
,, V.	Sirhowy	J. Hughes	G. A. Coates	—
,, VI.	Abercarn	E. Rogers	J. Bladin	W. Ratcliffe

The Abercarn Company disappears from the records after 1866, and mention is made in Regimental Orders, dated 14th May, 1868, of drills at Cwmbran. There were undoubtedly never less than six companies and it is probable that a new No. VI. Company was formed in 1867 in the district between Pontypool and Cwmbran, for references are made in later years to a company described variously at Panteg, Upper Pontnewydd and Cwmbran.

In 1877 a seventh company was raised at Garndiffaith, followed seven years later by one at Victoria. Changes made in the nomenclature and stations of companies resulted in the following distribution of the Battalion in 1884 :—

A Company,	Pontypool.	E Company,		Garndiffaith.
B	,,	Abersychan.	F ,,	Sirhowy.
C	,,	Ebbw Vale.	G ,,	Panteg.
D	,,	do.	H ,,	Victoria.

CHAPTER II.

3RD VOLUNTEER BATTALION
THE SOUTH WALES BORDERERS.
1885 – 1908.

THE adoption of the Cardwell scheme of Army reorganization, under which line regiments were linked together and designated by counties or districts, led in 1881 to the 24th (or 2nd Warwickshire) Regiment of Foot being named The South Wales Borderers, and to its depot being moved to Brecon, which became the headquarters of the 24th Regimental District. Following this, the 1st Breconshire and the 1st, 2nd and 3rd Monmouthshire Rifle Volunteer Corps were renamed in 1885 respectively the 1st, 2nd, 3rd and 4th Volunteer Battalions The South Wales Borderers.

The new 1st and 3rd Battalions already wore scarlet, and so far as the 3rd Battalion was concerned its green facings were altered to white in conformity with the new rule for the regular unit. Subsequently the whole regiment was permitted to change to the grass-green facings which the 24th Regiment had worn for two hundred years.

The Battalion suffered a grievous loss in 1887 through the assassination of its commanding officer, Colonel R. B. Roden, while travelling in Corsica. Founder of the Corps, he had commanded it during the whole 26 years of its existence, being junior at the time of his death to but one officer in the whole Volunteer Force. To quote from a Special Order announcing his death, " In Colonel Roden . . . the Battalion has lost a most able and efficient C.O., and one who, by his kind and genial manner and thoughtful consideration for the feelings of others, had won the esteem and regard of the whole regiment. He was . . . always enthusiastic, and, displaying considerable ability in the management of the Battalion's affairs and devotion to its interests, he spared no efforts to make it both in appearance and

3RD VOLUNTEER BATTALION S.W.B.

efficiency, a credit to the force to which it belongs." The whole Battalion was present at his funeral at Usk on the 16th April, and at a later date the officers placed a brass plate to his memory in St. Mary's Church.

Colonel Roden had played a notable part in developments and improvements to the rifle. He was associated with the patentee at the time of the conversion from the old muzzle-loading Enfield to the Snider breech-loader and held the Snider patent rights. Many of his experiments were carried out on the Battalion ranges.

He was succeeded in the command by Major and Honorary Lieutenant-Colonel T. Mitchell, who had served continuously in the Battalion since his first appointment as Ensign on 16th January, 1861, soon after the original Corps was formed. There have been many family ties with the Battalion, several sons having followed their fathers, but the Mitchell family connection is the most outstanding. Colonel Mitchell's two sons served under him, one of them being his second-in-command, and the family association is continued to-day in the person of his grandson, Major L. A. Mitchell.

In July, 1887, the Battalion was present at the Jubilee Review of Volunteers by Her Majesty QUEEN VICTORIA at Aldershot. This was the largest muster of the force up to that period, there being approximately 58,000 Volunteer troops present. The *Times*, commenting on the march past of the South Wales Borderers Brigade, said : " The brigade was preceded by two goats, one with gilt horns. The men of these four battalions were sturdy fellows, and their march past was undeniably excellent."

Major J. O. Carnegie retired on 2nd February, 1891, having held the appointment of adjutant for the record period of thirty years. His successor was Captain (now Brigadier-General) J. H. du B. Travers, 24th Regiment. The tenure of the adjutancy from this date onwards was limited to five years.

A new set of Rules* for the Battalion was issued in May, 1891. These show few variations of importance from the Rules of 1861, but the Committee to aid the Commanding Officer in financial matters under the new Rules was to be composed of officers only.

* See Appendix B.

Colonel T. MITCHELL
Commanding Officer 1887 - 1891.

3RD VOLUNTEER BATTALION S.W.B.

On 5th September, 1891, Colonel T. Mitchell retired and his elder son, Major B. M. Mitchell, temporarily assumed the duties of command. In Volunteer days appointment to command depended far more upon regimental officers than upon the authorities, the seal of whose approval was only sought when the officers were agreed. Considerable difficulty arose in finding a successor to Colonel Mitchell, and the minute book of the period shows that several gentlemen of the county were approached by deputations of officers and invited to accept the command, but without success.

Eventually Captain J. A. Bradney, Royal Monmouthshire Engineers (Militia), accepted the invitation and was appointed to command with the rank of Lieutenant-Colonel on 23rd April, 1892.

At the end of that year Lieutenant-Colonel Bradney issued his first Annual Circular Letter to all ranks, a custom which he kept up during the long period of his command. These letters recapitulated the year's events in the Battalion, and form a remarkable and reliable record. Unfortunately, the custom died out on his retirement and was not revived until 1929.

The keen interest in the Battalion which had always been evinced by the Hanbury family, of Pontypool Park, received recognition when Mr. J. C. Hanbury, then head of the family, was appointed Honorary Colonel on 29th October, 1892. The Park was always readily available to the local Volunteers, and besides much financial assistance, several cups and trophies had been presented by members of the family to the Battalion. In 1894, to celebrate the arrival of a son and heir, the Honorary Colonel gave a fete to the Battalion.

At the Queen's Diamond Jubilee celebrations in London on 22nd June, 1897, a detachment of 1 Sergeant and 20 Men under Captain D. S. Davies represented the Battalion, being stationed on Westminster Bridge during the procession.

Few events of note broke the quiet life of the Battalion until the stirring years of the South African War. Perusal of the record of General Meetings shows how life revolved round the annual camp, every effort being spent to make it a success. For a few years camps were regimental only, the site being selected at a meeting of officers. To Monmouthshire belongs the distinction of initiating Brigade Camps: the 1st, 2nd and 3rd Volunteer Battalions The South Wales Borderers camped together at Abergavenny Racecourse in 1886 under Colonel Campbell, commanding the 24th Regimental District, this being the first Brigade camp in the annals of the Volunteer Force.

Payment to the men for days of attendance at camp was introduced into the Battalion in 1893, the money being found from regimental funds. It is presumed that a certain amount of " skrimshanking " from parades existed, for in the following year the minute book records that " it was resolved that men at camp should be paid by cheques; paper cheques of different colours for each day are to be distributed by the Sergeant Instructors to the men each morning and collected when on parade."

THE SOUTH AFRICAN WAR,

1900 - 1902.

The outbreak of the Boer War in 1899 gave Volunteers an opportunity of active service, for the military authorities soon asked for men to serve in South Africa. No complete volunteer infantry units were despatched, but companies were formed at home which joined their affiliated regular battalions in the field. They served abroad for a year and were then relieved by a fresh company.

The whole 3rd Volunteer Battalion The South Wales Borderers expressed their readiness to proceed on active service if necessary, but only 1 Sergeant, 1 Corporal and 17 Men were permitted to join their comrades of the other three battalions in forming the 1st Volunteer Company. This contingent, under Sergeant A. Search, who was subsequently mentioned in despatches for gallantry in the field, was given a public send-off from Pontypool on 26th January, 1900, the beflagged streets being thronged with cheering people.

The Company joined the 2nd Battalion The South Wales Borderers at Osfontein on the 8th May, 1900, and were in action at the crossing of the Zand River two days later.

3RD VOLUNTEER BATTALION S.W.B.

The South African War developed early into a guerilla campaign, in which the highly organized British Army was engaged in rounding up swift-moving, semi-independent commandos of Boers, which had no bases or lines of communication to hamper them, and which subsisted mainly on the land and occasionally on the results of successful raids on our convoys or food-dumps.

The services of the 1st Volunteer Company are admirably summarized in the following Battalion Order issued by Lieut.-Colonel The Hon. U. de R. B. Roche, Commanding 2nd South Wales Borderers, dated Krugersdorp, 9th October, 1900 :—

" In bidding farewell and God-speed to the Volunteer Company of the Regiment on their departure for home, the Commanding Officer cannot allow such an event to pass without placing on record the magnificent services rendered by the Company during the entire time that they were with the 2nd Battalion in South Africa.

" The Company joined at Osfontein on the 8th May during the general advance of Lord Roberts' force upon the capital of the Transvaal, and took part in the action of Zand River and the taking of Johannesburg. After this they were employed with the Battalion in the defence of the railway line between Kroomellenberg and Rhenoster River, which was constantly subjected to attack by Commandant Christian de Wet ; here the duties of outposts, patrols and entrenching were extremely hard. The Battalion remained in defence of the line until Commandant de Wet was forced to cross the Vaal River to the north, when they were ordered to move rapidly to reinforce various parts on the line to the north, which were threatened by de Wet's force. They ultimately reached Krugersdorp on the 13th August, where they remained until August 30th, when they joined General Fitzroy Hart's column to operate in the Potchefstroom district against various Commandos of the enemy. For 30 days the Battalion was constantly on the move and covered 310 miles, including many forced marches by day and night, one of which measured 44 miles, and effected the reoccupation of Potchefstroom, and the capture of many of the enemy. 29 engagements were fought during this expedition, and the column was ordered back to Krugersdorp. In the performance of all these operations, the Battalion has served under five different Generals, and all have expressed their deepest admiration of the work done by the Battalion, and some have specially referred to the fine marching and soldier-like bearing of the Volunteer Company.

" The Commanding Officer on behalf of himself and the whole Regiment tenders his warmest thanks to the Officers, Non-Commissioned Officers and Men of the Volunteer Company for the manner in which they have at all times during this campaign served the Battalion ; and he assures them that it is with feelings of genuine regret that they bid them farewell, and it is the hope of all ranks, that if ever the Regiment is again called to active service, they will have the assistance of their old comrades of the South Wales Borderers Volunteers to uphold the fine traditions of the good old Regiment of which we are all so proud."

There were a few casualties among the 1st Volunteer Company, but none amongst the 3rd V.B. contingent.

A call for a 2nd Volunteer Company to replace the 1st again met with a ready response within the 3rd Battalion, which, owing to the other Volunteer units in the 24th Regimental District being unable to supply their quota of men, made up the numbers necessary to complete. Of the 2nd Company, 1 Officer, Captain H. L. Rosser, and 70 Rank and File were from the 3rd Battalion.

This Company landed at Cape Town on 16th April, 1901, and was sent to Beaufort West in Cape Colony. It was employed for a time on garrison and convoy duties and came into action first on the 4th July, when it beat off a Boer attack on Richmond. It did not join the 2nd South Wales Borderers until towards the middle of September.

The blockhouse system for the protection of lines of communication was by this time thoroughly developed, and the 2nd S.W.B. had been employed on a portion of the railway line in the vicinity of Klerksdorp since April. The Volunteer Company took their full share with the regular companies in the duties, the monotony of which was occasionally relieved by a Boer raid or by the formation of a flying column.

3RD VOLUNTEER BATTALION S.W.B.

A 3rd Volunteer Company, which included 14 men of the 3rd Volunteer Battalion, joined the 2nd South Wales Borderers on 15th April, 1902, being in time to see something of the preliminary parleys at Klerksdorp between the leaders of both sides, which led to the conclusion of hostilities on 31st May, 1902.

Including drafts, a total of 131 members of the 3rd Volunteer Battalion served with the 2nd South Wales Borderers during the war, and to them is due the distinction " South Africa, 1900-1902 " now borne on the Regimental Colour. The Battalion was singularly fortunate in that only one failed to return home : Sergeant R. Francis, who died of enteric, and to whose memory the officers placed a brass plate in Trevethin Parish Church. In addition to the active service detachments, Captains H. Griffiths and H. Charles, and Lieutenant Straker, served with the Imperial Yeomanry, the last-named in the ranks.

In the meantime the training of Volunteers at home had undergone radical changes. The camps of 1899 were the last in which training consisted principally of brigade ceremonial drill— a vast unit forming line, close column, wheeling and so forth— which, while a magnificent spectacle to the onlookers, was arduous work for the troops, and in the following years tactical training was given more prominence.

On one occasion, on which companies were representing skeleton battalions, a man of the Newbridge detachment was posted out and told he represented a company. Some time later an officer rode up and questioned him. The man of course mixed up his instructions and was duly lectured, his role being again explained. As the officer at last turned away, the man said, " Well, sir, if I'm a company, do I draw a company's beer when we get back to camp ?"

Training was naturally influenced by conditions in South Africa, and the escort of convoys was usually made a feature of the daily march from camp to the training areas. There being no transport vehicles, men were told off to represent them, until one day a man was found basking comfortably in the sun, while his comrades sweated up and down the sandhills, his explanation being that having lost a wheel he was awaiting repairs.

3RD VOLUNTEER BATTALION S.W.B.

In 1900 the Battalion had the honour of lining the streets of Monmouth on the occasion of a visit by the present KING and QUEEN (then DUKE and DUCHESS OF YORK).

The present headquarters drill hall at Pontypool was formally opened by the Honorary Colonel, Mr. J. C. Hanbury, on 20th December, 1902, in the presence, amongst others of Lord Tredegar, the Lord Lieutenant, who had been received by a guard of honour. After the ceremony Mr. Hanbury gave a lunch to the Volunteers in the Town Hall, at which the Lord Lieutenant presented medals to members of the Battalion who had earned them in South Africa.

On the occasion of the visit of His Majesty KING EDWARD VII. to Cardiff, on 13th July, 1907, the Battalion took a prominent part in the ceremonies. No official assistance being available, Colonel Bradney took the Battalion at his own expense. 24 Officers, and 786 Rank and File paraded and were given the duty of lining St. Mary's Street for the royal procession. They then moved to Castle Street, which was lined for the King's visit to Caerphilly, and subsequently returned to St. Mary's Street for His Majesty's progress to the station.

While in camp in 1907, the Battalion had the honour of entertaining the Right Hon. R. B. (afterwards Lord) Haldane, then Secretary of State for War, who came at the invitation of Colonel Bradney and the Officers. He inspected companies in their working clothes in the afternoon of 23rd July and presented a few Long Service Medals. On the following morning, after inspecting the Brigade, he delivered his famous speech indicating the general lines on which the Territorial Force was to be founded.

The first change in the distribution of companies from the days of the 2nd Monmouthshire Rifle Volunteer Corps took place in 1891, when " G " Company was transferred from Panteg to Abersychan. This appears, however, to have been no more than an interchange of names with " C " Company, whose station is described up to 1899 as Upper Pontnewydd and subsequently as Cwmbran.

In 1892 and 1895 permission was sought to raise companies at Crumlin and Abertillery respectively, but was refused. In 1897, however, sanction was given to establish a detachment at Abertillery, and the headquarters of " H " Company were moved there from Victoria.

3RD VOLUNTEER BATTALION S.W.B.

From 1900 to 1908 the Battalion had never less than nine companies, and for two of these years it had ten. In 1900 " I " Company was raised at Abercarn, one of the original stations which had been abandoned for many years, and in 1901 " K " Company was formed at Ebbw Vale. " K " was a Cyclist Company, but difficulties in keeping it up to strength were experienced, and in 1903 it was abandoned. During these years the Battalion was extremely strong, the peak year being 1901, when its membership was 1,172 all ranks, this being well over the establishment.

In the middle 'nineties, the Battalion did exceptionally well in musketry. It gained second place in the Western District (*i.e.*, South Wales, Somersetshire, Devon and Cornwall) in 1894, and occupied first place for the three following years, as well as providing each year the best individual shot. In 1904 it was again first in the Western District.

CHAPTER III.

2ND BATTALION
THE MONMOUTHSHIRE REGIMENT (T.F.)
1908 - 1914.

A FUNDAMENTAL defect of the Volunteer Force from the viewpoint of national security was that it was not so organized that it could take the field in fighting formations in the event of war. It consisted mainly of infantry, and there were a few units of other arms, especially artillery, but the highest formation was only an infantry brigade, the command of which was but an *ex-officio* appointment of the Officer Commanding a Regimental District. There were no fixed establishments, and even the number of companies varied in different units. Another important deficiency was that, while no doubt existed as to the willingness, even anxiety, of the force to serve in time of war, the Government had no legal power to mobilize it. Here was a great unwieldy mass of valuable material requiring organization and control before it could be considered an efficient striking weapon.

To place the national second line of defence in a state of preparedness a new army was required, one which would replace the Volunteers while preserving their spirit, and in 1908 the Territorial Force was inaugurated for this purpose. Complete divisions were formed, with staffs, infantry, cavalry and artillery, and with engineer, signal, medical, transport and supply services, similar in organization, arms, and equipment to divisions of the Regular Army. Officers desirous of continuing were to be granted fresh commissions, men were to be formally attested instead of enrolled, and all were made liable to turn out when required for the defence of the United Kingdom.

Full advantage was taken of existing organisms, in order that continuity should not be broken, and in the hope, very largely realized, that Volunteers would flock to the new force.

Colonel Sir JOSEPH BRADNEY, c.b., t.d., d.l.
Commanding Officer 1892 - 1911.
Honorary Colonel since 1922.

2ND BATTALION THE MONMOUTHSHIRE REGIMENT (T.F.)

At the same time unit's recruiting areas were defined, thus ending the overlapping through which Pontypool, for example, was shared by two battalions.

This last-mentioned reform was responsible for a vast upheaval among the three Monmouthshire battalions, which took the opportunity, amid the general post, to return to their old name of Monmouthshire Regiment, thus securing closer identity with their county than the generic title South Wales Borderers implies.

The 3rd V.B. S.W.B., renamed 2nd Battalion The Monmouthshire Regiment, lost four of its nine companies, one, Cwmbran, going to the new 1st Battalion, and three, Ebbw Vale, Sirhowy and Abertillery, to the new 3rd Battalion. In exchange it was given three companies from the old 4th Volunteer Battalion, at Pontypool, Blaenavon and Monmouth (with Usk) respectively. At the same time new companies were raised at Llanhilleth and Crumlin, the men at Newbridge, which ceased to be a station, being granted the opportunity of absorption into the Crumlin company.

The obligations of officers and men as Territorials were greatly increased. In addition to the musketry course, 20 drills instead of 9 had to be performed, and annual training of 15 days in camp to be attended, in exchange for which, however, they were to receive pay and allowances at military rates while in camp.

The new force was from the first extremely popular, and, while a few Volunteers were unable to accept the new conditions, the numbers were soon made up by recruits. The 2nd Monmouthshires dropped from a strength of 1,043 Volunteers in 1907 to 783 Territorials in 1908, but it should be noted that the outgoing companies were nearly 200 stronger than those which came into the Battalion. The following year the strength rose to 946, and it remained over 900 up to 1914.

The chief event of 1909 was the presentation of Colours to the Battalion by His Majesty KING EDWARD VII., at Windsor, on the 19th June. A detachment of Officers, N.C.O.'s and Men was present and witnessed the impressive ceremony, a large number of other Territorial units receiving their Colours on the

2ND BATTALION THE MONMOUTHSHIRE REGIMENT (T.F.)

same occasion. The Battalion Colour Party consisted of Second Lieutenants H. W. E. Bailey and E. D. T. Jenkins with Colour-Sergeants Humphreys, Tew and Edwards. The King's Colour comprises the Union Jack, with a circle inscribed II. The Monmouthshire Regiment, surmounted by a Royal Crown.

The Regimental Colour is of dark green silk, with a circle in the centre inscribed similarly to that on the King's Colour, but surrounded by the Union Wreath (the Rose, Thistle and Shamrock). Underneath is the old Battalion motto, "*Gwell Angau Na Gwarth*" (Rather Death Than Dishonour), and the first battle honour "South Africa 1900-02," below which is a Tudor rose. There have since been added the ten honours awarded for the Great War.

The old Colours, presented by ladies of the county in 1861, were retired and deposited in Trevethin Parish Church, where they now hang in the Battalion Memorial Chapel.

A detachment of 25 N.C.O.'s and Men under Major J. C. Jenkins attended the coronation of Their Majesties KING GEORGE V. and QUEEN MARY, in London, on 22nd June, 1911. They formed part of a battalion composed of similar representative parties from all T.F. battalions in the Western Command, the whole being under the command of Colonel Bradney.

On 13th July of the same year, 13 Officers and 300 Men represented the Battalion at the investiture of H.R.H. The PRINCE OF WALES at Carnarvon Castle, Colonel Bradney being again in command of a composite battalion.

Lieutenant-Colonel and Hon. Colonel J. A. Bradney, who had been created C.B., retired on 26th April, 1911. He had commanded the Battalion for twenty years, had brought it to a high state of efficiency in Volunteer days, and had piloted it successfully into the Territorial Army. In its fifty-fourth year of existence, Colonel Bradney was only its third Commanding Officer.

He was succeeded by Lieutenant-Colonel C. B. Cuthbertson, M.V.O., a retired regular officer who had seen service in the South African War with the Argyll and Sutherland Highlanders. A keen Scotsman, he was destined to lead one of the first Welsh Territorial Battalions into active service.

2ND BATTALION THE MONMOUTHSHIRE REGIMENT (T.F.)

In 1914 the Battalion was to have taken part in Army manœuvres on a grand scale, arranged to take place in the area Herefordshire, Gloucestershire and Wiltshire, but real war intervened.

Orders to mobilize the Battalion were received at about 5 p.m. on the 5th August. They were at once transmitted to the detachments, and on the following day the whole Battalion entrained for its war station at Pembroke Dock. Considering how the Battalion was scattered over Monmouthshire, this was a performance which marks the excellence of the arrangements made beforehand. It is true that the few days of the precautionary period, which preceded the actual orders to mobilize, permitted final adjustment of details, but the rapidity with which our civilian army gathered for the fray showed that their organization compared not unfavourably with that of the regular army.

The following description, by C.S.M. C. E. Edwards, will revive memories of the apparently hectic confusion which frothed on top, concealing the soundness of the organization beneath:
" I was warned by the local police sergeant on Bank Holiday Tuesday to proceed at once to my Drill Hall, Crumlin, for embodiment. Most of the men of my company turned up, the few absentees being men away on holiday. I had no company officer, he being away on his honeymoon, having been married on the previous Saturday. The men were kept at the Drill Hall until about 11.30 p.m., when Colonel Cuthbertson arrived and gave permission for all to return to their homes for the night, but to parade again at 6 next morning.

" This time nearly the whole company asembled and it became a trying time keeping the men under restraint in the Drill Hall. Sentries were posted on all doors, but the Hall was besieged all day by relatives and friends, besides any number of would-be recruits, anxious to fight the Kaiser. It was not until the evening that a definite order as to the time of entraining came through, but about 7.30 p.m. the Company entrained at Crumlin nearly 100 strong, *en route* for Pembroke Dock.

Arrangements made for the camp at Pembroke Dock by the authorities responsible left a great deal to be desired. The men slept 22 in a tent, and had only biscuits and " bully " to eat.

2ND BATTALION THE MONMOUTHSHIRE REGIMENT (T.F.)

For four days no one had a wash, and to add to the discomfort heavy rains set in. No one grumbled, however—this was WAR."

On August 10th, the Battalion joined its Brigade (the Welsh Border) in camp at Oswestry, where hard training was at once commenced.

While arrangements for mobilizing the men were above praise, the plans for providing Territorial units with, amongst other things, transport proved inadequate. Unsuitable horses and vehicles were purchased owing to lack of experience in military requirements, and echoes of the laughter with which the Pontypool Urban District Council water-cart was greeted on its arrival at Oswestry have not yet died away. This vehicle was admirably suited for keeping the dust down, but it had been seized for duty as a regimental water-cart.

The horses and wagons impressed for the 2nd Monmouthshires were collected in Pontypool Park in the afternoon of the 7th August, collecting parties having been left behind by the Battalion. The transport moved off the same evening, and, halting for the nights at Llanelen, Hereford, Ludlow and Church Stretton, completed the march to Oswestry on the afternoon of the 11th August, a distance of nearly 110 miles in four days.

On 20th August, the Brigade moved to Northampton, where the Welsh Division was concentrating. Here training was intensified, and the whole machinery of the Battalion overhauled. The medically unfit were weeded out and their places filled by recruits. The Battalion was fortunate in having an unusually large number of old soldiers in its ranks, and its discipline and training were consequently of a high standard. It changed without waiting for authority to the four-company system which had been adopted earlier in the year in the Regular Army but which had not yet reached the Territorials.

In the early days of the war there were constant alarms of impending German landings on the East Coast, and as a result of one of these the Battalion was rushed with little warning, on September 29th, to Ipswich, to dig trenches. It had hardly settled into billets, however, before it was ordered back to Northampton to re-equip and get ready to proceed overseas at

BRIGADIER-GENERAL E. B. CUTHBERTSON, C.M.G., M.V.O.
Commanding Officer 1911 - 1915.

2ND BATTALION THE MONMOUTHSHIRE REGIMENT (T.F.)

short notice. To be selected as one of the first Territorial battalions to reinforce the hard-tried remnants of the original Expeditionary Force in France was a signal honour, which is eloquent of the high state of efficiency to which Colonel Cuthbertson had brought the 2nd Monmouthshires.

After a strenuous month of training and overhauling, the Battalion embarked at Southampton on the evening of 5th November, 1914, on the " Manchester Importer," which arrived off Le Havre the following afternoon and anchored in the harbour until night.

On the departure to Northampton a second line battalion of the 2nd Monmouthshires had been raised, and later a third was formed, of which some notes are furnished later in this book. To distinguish between units, the original Battalion became the 1/2nd Monmouthshires, and the others the 2/2nd and 3/2nd respectively.

CHAPTER IV.

THE FIRST WINTER IN FLANDERS—MINING—"YPRES, 1915"—THE AMALGAMATED REGIMENT—THE SOMME IN 1915—LINES OF COMMUNICATION DUTIES.

THE FIRST WINTER IN FLANDERS.

THE 7th November, 1914, is an historic date for the 2nd Monmouthshires, for early on the morning of that day the Battalion landed at Havre on active service. Over four long and terrible years were to drag their slow length before it would recross the narrow sea from France, and few of those who disembarked with it were fated to return with it. Its strength on landing was 30 Officers and 984 Other Ranks. Before it came home 180 Officers and 3,878 Other Ranks had passed through it. But they had earned for their Battalion a name for fighting and endurance of which their county, with all its old traditions of border pugnacity, could well be proud. While some of the officers came from other counties, a few indeed from the colonies and abroad, the vast majority of the men were from the mining valleys of Monmouthshire, every town, village and hamlet of which must at one time or another have been represented in the 2nd Battalion.

The 2nd Monmouthshire was one of the six Territorial battalions awarded the 1914 Star, and it gained several distinctions unique in the Territorial Army. It was the first Territorial unit to enter the trenches, and the first to be entrusted with holding a battalion sector of the line; one of its members, Corporal J. Pinchin, received the first fighting decoration ever awarded to a Territorial soldier; and at the end of the War it was the only Territorial battalion to march into Germany.

The Battalion entrained on the 8th November and arrived at St. Omer after a tedious journey of two days in the uncomfortable trucks marked " Hommes 40—Chevaux 8," with which the war-time generation of soldiers was to become familiar.

From St. Omer a march was made to Wizerne where a week was spent in strenuous training within sound of the guns. During their stay at Wizerne the veteran Field-Marshal Lord Roberts, v.c., died at St. Omer, and the Battalion had the melancholy honour of being represented on the escort when the great soldier's remains were conveyed to the railway station.

On the 18th and 19th the Battalion, having been inspected and passed fit by the Inspector of Reserve Troops, marched to Bailleul, halting for the night at Hazebrouck, and on the following day it reached Le Bizet, coming under the command of the G.O.C., 12th Infantry Brigade, 4th Division, and being at last in the fighting zone.

On 21st November " C " and " D " Companies entered the trenches for instruction under the 2nd Lancashire Fusiliers and 2nd Essex Regiment. The Battalion suffered its first casualty on the following day, Private Crowley of " C " Company being shot and killed by a German sniper. "A" and " B " Companies relieved " C " and " D" on the 23rd, and this system of instruction in trench occupation, routine and relief, continued under the guidance of the two regular units until the Battalion was considered sufficiently " blooded " to trench warfare to hold the sector independently. Another man was killed and three wounded by snipers during these ten days of instruction.

The two companies not in the line " rested," that is to say they worked all night on trench construction and repair and rested during the day. Second Lieutenant C. Comely describes the first working party as follows : " We were guided to our work on the 21st November by a captain of the Essex Regiment. The bit of trench allotted to my platoon, No. 8, was just behind our front line and about 100 yards from the Boche. We arrived just before dark and on being told we were not in view climbed over the top. After setting out two or three pairs of men to dig, our officer guide received a bullet in the elbow and had to leave us. Fairly active sniping was kept up by the enemy, so we waited till darkness hid us. This was our first time under fire and, although new to the game, the men behaved like old soldiers. The work was completed to the tune of bullets hitting the old pollard withies under which the trench was made."

THE FIRST WINTER IN FLANDERS

The 2nd Monmouthshires relieved the 2nd Essex on the 2nd December, taking over a battalion frontage of eleven hundred yards of trenches between the railway, where it crossed the Frelinghein-Le Ghier road, and the Warnave Stream, about three miles north-west of Armentieres on the Franco-Belgian frontier. Corporal J. Pinchin, of Talywain, and Private E. Jones, of Pontypool, were both awarded D.C.M.'s for acts of conspicuous gallantry in this first week, Pinchin being the first Territorial to receive a decoration in the field.

The same trenches were occupied until 6th January, 1915, the Battalion alternating with the 2nd Essex every four days. The Essex men, mainly Londoners, particularly admired the dexterity with pick and spade of their Monmouthshire comrades, and the Battalion surprised its Generals by its ingenuity in constructing dugouts and improving the trenches. It comprised nearly eighty per cent. miners, men who live on the pick and spade, and amongst its officers were several mining engineers. When these facts became known, a detachment under Captain A. H. Edwards was drawn from the unit for mining operations.

Very heavy rains fell during December, and owing to the flatness of the ground drainage of the trenches was extremely difficult. Traffic along the communication trenches became at times impossible owing to their flooded condition, and reliefs and ration parties could frequently approach only " over the top " by night. All available men were constantly employed in trying to keep the trenches dry, some pumps and vast quantities of brushwood and planks being supplied for the purpose. But conditions at the best were deplorable, and the sick list was correspondingly large, many men being affected by frostbite, and many more by a new disease, developed under these wet conditions, commonly known as " trench-feet."

Christmas Day, 1914, was spent in the front line. "A" Company greeted the dawn by singing seasonable anthems with all the gusto which Welshmen can put into such cheery harmonies. A sheet of the *Pontypool Free Press* was then tied to a rifle and waved over the top as a flag of truce. The enemy opposite, the 7th Bavarians, were equally ready to have a holiday, and sat on top of their trenches, fifty yards off, waving and making signs of friendliness. Several men went over with bully beef and cigarettes, and souvenirs were exchanged. Later in the morning, however, a sergeant of " D " Company, returning from giving tobacco was shot and killed, and the informal truce came to an abrupt end. At other parts of the line the Germans waved the Monmouthshires to go back and get under cover, evidently under orders that intercourse must cease. Subsequent Christmas Days were marked only by the cessation of artillery fire, fraternization with the enemy being sternly forbidden.

Early in January, 1915, a redistribution of troops resulted in a reduction of the brigade frontage, and in order to permit of frequent reliefs, battalion sectors were narrowed to permit of one company only being in the front line, with a second in support, while the remaining two rested in dry billets. The forward company of the 2nd Monmouthshires, which was relieved every two days, held some cottages and about eighty yards of trench behind Le Ghier Wood, running north-west from the railway. The weather remained steadily bad, and constant pumping was required to keep the water in the trenches down. The support and reserve companies were fully employed in trying to keep the trenches in order and in constructing a second line.

On one occasion, while resting from the trenches, part of the Battalion had gone to a flax-washing factory outside Armentieres for baths and change of clothing. " B " Company were bathing in big tubs when, unexpectedly, HIS MAJESTY THE KING, accompanied by the PRINCE OF WALES and Field-Marshal SIR JOHN FRENCH, smilingly walked in. This was probably the least informal inspection the Battalion will ever have to undergo, and C.S.M. Edwards says it was a treat to see the looks on the faces of the men, who were attired of course as soldiers usually are when bathing on active service.

The Battalion relieved the 2nd Essex on 20th February, taking over the same frontage occupied in December, and from that date to the end of March the two regiments relieved each other regularly every four days in practically the same sector.

Lieutenant-Colonel Cuthbertson, Captain H. J. Miers, Second Lieutenant J. E. Paton, R.S.M. J. Noble and Sergeant F. Collins were mentioned in dispatches at the end of February, the Commanding Officer being awarded also the C.M.G., while the R.S.M. received the M.C.

THE FIRST WINTER IN FLANDERS

Although no engagements had been fought up to the end of March, there had been a steady toll of casualties, which on the 30th had risen to 4 Officers killed and 6 wounded, and 32 Other Ranks killed and 125 wounded, considerably exceeding the strength of a complete company of to-day. The first officer to lose his life was Second Lieutenant J. E. Paton, shot on the 31st December. He was a son of Mr. John Paton, of Pontypool, an old officer of the Battalion, and no finer epitaph can be given him than that by one of his men : " He wouldn't ask you to take a risk that he wouldn't take himself. If there was anything to be done, he'd do it. He was a champion officer."

The other officers were Captain V. H. Watkins, who died on 20th February of wounds received a month earlier, Second Lieutenant C. A. H. Hillier, who died of wounds on 27th February, and Lieutenant J. W. Taylor, who was killed on the 11th March. A brother officer writes of Taylor : " He was killed when he had voluntarily taken my platoon up into the line to give me a rest, an act which was typical of him. By his devotion to duty and unselfish care of his men he had endeared himself to all ranks. A better soldier never commanded men, and his death was a loss which is still felt."

As winter passed, the sick numbers decreased, but one-third of the officers and men had been constantly absent through illness, involuntarily throwing an increasing burden on their comrades. This is a casualty state which is its own comment on the severity of the conditions. Trenches of the first winter in Flanders were at their best but ditches, and at their worst channels of water and slimy mud. A hole scratched in the side of a trench provided precarious shelter from shell and weather : the men had no means of keeping dry and few of keeping warm.

April found the Battalion still in the Le Bizet area, and on the 18th, Second Lieutenant R. B. Comely was badly wounded by a rifle grenade. He had previously distinguished himself in connection with directing the fire of a trench mortar on certain of the enemy's earthworks and was later awarded the M.C. A day or so later the Division was withdrawn from the line for a rest.

There was in " B " Company in these days a man whose identity may be recognized under his nickname of " Trousers."

He was one of the dull, dirty type which breaks a sergeant-major's heart, and was naturally shuttle-cocked about from one job to another—anything was better than having him with the Company. Once he got fired out of a job as groom when the Company was in the line, and fume as he might, the Company Sergeant-Major had no option but to keep him. During the night when his turn of sentry duty came, the platoon sergeant posted " Trousers " himself, and feeling that the less he said the less chance there would be of instructions being muddled, he reduced the orders to : " Keep your eyes peeled, and if anything moves, shoot."

After some little time had elapsed, like everyone else who has stood gazing from a fire-step at night, "Trousers" thought he saw something moving. He bobbed below the parapet, elevated his rifle to an angle of 45 degrees, let fly the whole magazine, climbed up again, and shouted triumphantly towards Germany, " Now go away and bandage your b——y heads up ! "

MINING.

As has been mentioned earlier, a detachment was drawn from the Battalion in December, 1914, for mining operations. It consisted of Captain (afterwards Major) A. H. Edwards, 2 N.C.O.'s and 12 Men, and was called the 4th Divisional Mining Party. In January it was reinforced by a few men from the 5th South Lancashires.

Work was commenced in conditions which the C.R.E. of the Division described as making mining impossible, and certainly their first mine had to be given up when the trenches in its neighbourhood became waterlogged.

The second mine was successful, however, despite all difficulties. It was commenced from the cellar of a house a few yards behind the front line, the objective being a row of cottages behind the German forward trenches at Le Touquet. These were suspected of being used as billets and known to harbour some troublesome snipers. When about 500 feet of the mine had been dug, the enemy was heard counter-mining. A branch shaft was run out about 50 feet in their direction, in

MINING

which two men were constantly stationed, alternately listening for the enemy and striking stones with an entrenching tool to deceive him. Meanwhile work in the mine proper continued, and it was eventually charged with 30 bags of gunpowder and 24 boxes of gun-cotton and tamped. Then early one morning in March the artillery bombarded for an hour, and at 8 a.m. the mine was fired. Half a dozen of the group of houses went up in the air, and the casualties must have been heavy. This was the first British mine blown in the War.

During the same period the 4th Divisional Mining Party dug a mine from Railway Barricade. The enemy counter-mined and broke on 28th February into the work, and a fierce underground hand to hand fight ensued, in which the Germans were eventually worsted. Before evacuating their works they fired a gas grenade, killing one man, the only casualty suffered by the Mining Party.

Captain Edwards received the congratulations of the G.O.C. for the success of the party, and was awarded the M.C., while Sergeant Yates and Privates Lewis and Morgan received the D.C.M.

Soon after this the Mining Party was broken up on the formation of Tunnelling Companies, and the men returned to the Battalion in time for the battles in May.

"YPRES, 1915."

The 4th Division was out of the line resting in the Bailleul area when the series of actions, known collectively as the Second Battle of Ypres, commenced. The 2nd Mons. in the 12th Brigade consequently missed the first phase, the Battle of Gravenstafel Ridge of 22nd and 23rd April, although the other two brigades were in action before the fight ended. This was the occasion when the Germans first used poisonous gas which, put down on French colonial and territorial troops, enabled them to gain ground on the left of the British, who were hard put to it to cover the exposed flank.

The 2nd Mons. were present at the remaining actions and share with the two other battalions of the Regiment the battle

HIGH COMMAND TRENCH & SAP
CENTRAL FARM
LT. J. A. BURGOYNE ON FIRESTEP.

SNIPER'S COTTAGE
LE TOUQUET.

TOILET.

CAPT. A. EDWARDS' MINING PARTY.

Capt. A. J. H. Bowen.

Yser Canal
Ypres Burning in distance.

Front Line Trench, 1915.

Pontoon Bridge over Yser.

"YPRES, 1915"

honours, "Ypres 1915," "St. Julien," "Frezenberg" and "Bellewaarde," of which the two former are borne on the Regimental Colour.

The Battle of St. Julien raged from 24th April to 4th May, and the 4th Division was moved north to support the hard-pressed line. On the night of April 27th, the Battalion was billeted in Hazebrouck, where it rested for the day, moving after dark into bivouacs at Elverdinghe. On 30th April, the 12th Brigade, advancing over the Yser Canal after dusk under heavy fire, took over the left sector of the British line, the 2nd Monmouthshires going into reserve at La Brique.

Soon after daybreak on 2nd May, the 2nd Mons. experienced the heaviest shelling they had till then encountered, and later in the day the enemy launched a fierce attack under cover of asphyxiating gas. Overcome by the gas, against which protection in those days was very elementary, the Essex lost a portion of their line on Pilkem Ridge. Orders were sent to "B" and "C" Companies to send three platoons each to reinforce the Essex, but the message never reached "B" Company. "C" Company, under Captain A. J. H. Bowen, advanced in extremely good order under a terrific hail of shrapnel and reached the support line. In the meantime the Essex had regained their front positions, but retained "C" Company in support. Two platoons of "B" Company went forward later to reinforce the Royal Irish Regiment, but the action quietened down about 10 p.m. on the brigade front.

The Battalion relieved the 5th South Lancashires about Weiltje during the night of the 4th/5th May, just in time for a heavy gas attack which was, however, not followed up by an infantry assault. The position included Mouse Trap Farm, a place of considerable importance, as is shown by the following note, copied from German records of the fighting from 4th to 7th May, 1915: "On the front of the XXVI. Reserve Corps, Weiltje Chateau (Mouse Trap Farm) surrounded by its 10-feet moat, was recognised as an important strong-point. Heavy howitzer fire was concentrated on it, yet surprise attacks against it on the 6th and 7th failed."

The attack on the 7th coincided with an inter-company relief, and those going out had barely reached the reserve trenches when they were ordered back to the firing line. To do this they had to advance a considerable distance under continous shell fire, but the enemy failed in his effort, heavy casualties being inflicted on him.

During these struggles a shell, pitching through the roof of Mouse Trap Farm (which was also known to the British for a time as Shell Trap Farm), put all the Officers and N.C.O.'s out of action. Drummer " Danny " White swam across the moat, reached headquarters and reported the situation. He was told to return with the order that the survivors were to hold on at all costs. He managed to get back unscathed, and the Farm held out. White was later awarded the D.C.M. and the French Croix de Guerre.

Private Hemmings received the D.C.M. after this action for his gallantry in rescuing a wounded sergeant under particularly heavy fire, and for devotedly carrying out his duties as a stretcher bearer throughout the battle.

Heavy casualties were incurred during this fighting, and amongst the officers, Captain I. E. M. Watkins and Lieutenants A. E. Fraser and H. J. Walters were killed, while Captain Bowen and Lieutenants Byrde and S. R. Hockaday were wounded.

By the 8th May the British had withdrawn from the most advanced points of the Ypres salient, and the Germans, striving to obliterate the salient completely, made further determined efforts to gain ground. Desperate fighting ensued, the six days, 8th to 13th May, of the Battle of Frezenberg Ridge, giving many anxious hours to the British commanders. When the storm broke the Battalion was on the right of the brigade still holding Mouse Trap Farm, but the main attack being further south the brigade had no difficulty in holding its line. Indeed, normal routine was possible, in the course of which the Battalion was relieved on the night of the 8/9th by the Royal Irish, and went back to La Brique in reserve.

Fighting died down on the 13th, and on the 20th the Battalion went back with the Brigade to rest at Vlamertinghe, from which place parties were supplied for work on the new defences being constructed astride the St. Jean-Weiltje road.

On 24th May the enemy made what turned out to be his final effort to reach Ypres in 1915, the battle receiving the name of "Bellewaarde Ridge." The Battalion was in support about half a mile south east of Weiltje when the attack opened. Assisted by gas, the Germans captured Mouse Trap Farm, now a heap of mud and rubbish, and the forward positions rapidly became untenable in spite of counter-attacks. The 2nd Mons. were employed in digging a trench on which the forward troops could rally, and which eventually became the front line. On the evening of the 24th, active operations on the Divisional sector ceased, for the German battalions were equally as worn by the long struggle as were the British.

This brief account of Second Ypres does scant justice to the terrible conditions of strain and fatigue to which all ranks were put. Day after day they were pounded by the German guns, always threatened and frequently attacked by poisonous gas, often beating back the enemy with the bayonet, with never a chance of rest for days on end, for there was always a trench to be dug or repaired and no time to waste. This was a time when discipline told: officers and men stayed where they were put, and the 2nd Monmouthshires went through a trial which proved of the greatest value in later stages of the war.

The Battalion shared with the other regiments engaged the congratulations of the G.O.C. for their "superb bravery and resourcefulness in repelling the attacks and in confronting clouds of poisonous gases." Captains Bowen and Pennymore subsequently received the D.S.O. and C.S.M. Love the D.C.M. for their gallant leadership in the course of these fights.

About the middle of May the Battalion lost its C.O. Lieutenant-Colonel Cuthbertson was wounded and invalided home, where later he commanded a reserve brigade. He had shown himself a real friend to all young officers, and amid the worries and responsibilities that are the lot of a commanding officer, he yet found time to give them a guiding, helpful hand. He had always insisted on the care of the men being the first thought of the officers, and the reputation which the 2nd Monmouthshires built up was largely due to his efforts and inspiration in their first days of active service.

A week later the Battalion left the 4th Division for a time and, in bidding them farewell, Major-General Wilson, the G.O.C., said that he hoped the Division had lost them but

"YPRES, 1915"

temporarily, adding: "Your magnificent work in mining at Le Touquet and the Railway Barricade attracted the attention of the whole Army. On arriving in the Division you took your place with the Regular battalions of the 12th Brigade and you did your work as well as any of them. Since coming up here your endurance has been magnificent under very trying times. The 4th Division always knew when the line was held by the 2nd Mons. that that line was safe."

THE AMALGAMATED REGIMENT.

The 1st and 3rd Battalions The Monmouthshire Regiment, which arrived in France in February, had suffered terribly heavy casualties during the Second Battle of Ypres, more especially during the main German attack of the 9th of May. The 2nd Battalion, under Captain E. Edwards, was by now reduced to little more than half its establishment, and orders were received for the three battalions to amalgamate until such time as drafts would enable them to reform separately. Their strengths when they came together at Vlamertinghe Woods on May 27th were as follows :—

    1st Battalion : 11 Officers, 218 Other Ranks.
    2nd   ,,   19   ,,   580   ,,   ,,
    3rd   ,,   11   ,,   250   ,,   ,,

The amalgamated battalion was styled "The Monmouthshire Regiment," and Major W. S. Bridge, 3rd Battalion, was appointed to command. Brought about by the vicissitudes and calamities of war, the amalgamation had the happiest results in cementing the friendship between the three units.

The Monmouthshires were attached to the 84th Brigade of the 28th Division, and the period May 28th to June 10th was spent at Herzeele re-equipping the men, organizing companies, and in training. No attempt was made to keep the original units apart, but all "A" Company men of the three battalions were brought into the new "A" Company, and the other companies were formed similarly.

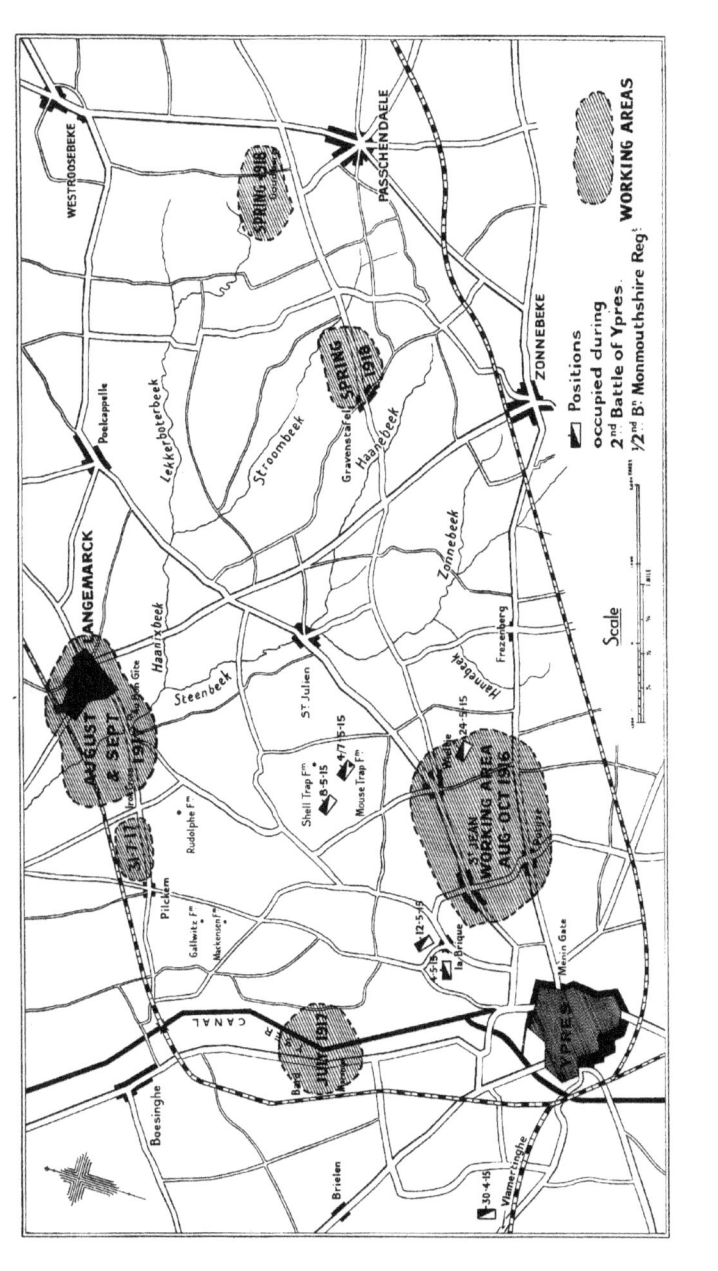

THE AMALGAMATED REGIMENT

On June 11th the Regiment marched to Renninghelst and on the following day to Dickebusch, where they relieved the 7th K.R.R. in the trenches in front of the Bois Carre, southeast of St. Eloi. Trench tours were now seven days in the line followed by seven in reserve, and the Monmouthshires had three visits to the same sector before the Brigade went back to Divisional reserve. This part of the line at that period was comparatively quiet and was on the whole considered a pleasant change. Casualties were incurred, of course, as part of the daily routine, but a great deal of improvement work was performed, especially by night parties, when the Monmouthshires were in Brigade reserve. Sports were held on 9th July.

The Regiment was billeted at Westoutre from July 15th to 19th, and then relieved the 1st Welsh in the trenches in front of Mount Kemmel, opposite Wytschaete, taking with it for instructional purposes a company of the 6th Welsh, near neighbours when at home. Although subjected to periods of active shelling, no casualties were sustained during this tour which was abruptly terminated on the 22nd to allow of the detachment of 2nd Battalion personnel.

The 1st and 3rd were to remain together a little longer, but on 23rd July the 2nd Monmouthshires paraded at Locre under Captain E. Edwards and left by train to rejoin the 4th Division.

THE SOMME IN 1915.

The 4th Division was now in the Somme district north of Albert, an area with which the Battalion was to become thoroughly familiar in later years, and in which the Division had succeeded French troops as holders of the line. Entraining at Godewaersvelde on July 24th, the 2nd Mons. arrived at Doullens in the early hours of the 25th and marched to Louvencourt, where a day was spent in re-organization. Thence, halting for a day at Forceville, where they found themselves again amongst old friends of the 12th Brigade, they marched to Auchonvillers, which they reached at night. Captain A. J. H. Bowen, D.S.O., rejoined here with a small draft and took over

THE SOMME IN 1915

command temporarily. He was followed a few days later by a further draft of officers and men to replace some of the losses which the Battalion had suffered at Ypres.

Auchonvillers stood about 800 yards behind the front line on the crest of a ridge overlooking the German positions. The sector had evidently been a quiet one while in French hands, for the " flimsy " state of the trenches proved that they had not been occupied by men often subjected to shell fire or attack, and the wire in front was very thin. On arrival in the village it was found that four cottages were still occupied by their peasant owners: they were quickly evacuated. All the other buildings were deserted, having been knocked about by shell fire and partly demolished. Headquarters was established in the centre of the village and the junior officers messed in a cottage close to the cross-roads. The Battalion's duty was to turn the village into a strong point, which, commanding a wide all-round field of fire, could be held if the lines in front were broken. Companies were allotted sectors for work, and as the weather was excellent and the Germans only fired salvos of " whizz-bangs " three times a day at regular hours, the commencement of the Battalion's occupation proved a welcome relief to those who were weary from the conflict at Ypres.

As time permitted the companies also cleaned and fortified the cellars and constructed dug-outs, finding the few remaining glass windows of the houses and the furniture and cutlery, abandoned by the French peasants, extremely useful in making themselves comfortable. It had been customary in digging new trenches to start work at a given time and to continue until the hour fixed for work to cease, but the experiment was tried in this village of allotting tasks to platoons, and permitting them to dismiss the moment the work was finished. The result was most successful, for in the first two or three days the men worked like niggers to finish their objective, the stronger willingly helping the weaker, and consequently the tasks were brought up to a stage commensurate with the men's abilities. Thus were laid the seeds of the rapid trench digging by which the men afterwards earned fame for the Battalion and the congratulations of all superiors under whom they were placed.

THE SOMME IN 1915

Lieutenant-Colonel J. C. Jenkins arrived from home on 13th August to take over the Battalion. He was invalided, however, on 5th September, and Captain Bowen succeeded to the command, this time with the rank of the appointment.

During August, mining was commenced in No Man's Land, some forty men of the Battalion being attached to a R.E. Tunnelling Company. It was known that the enemy was carrying out underground operations towards a position known as the Redan, and the 2nd Mons. mining party under Captain A. H. Edwards, M.C., made counter-preparations. On August 30th, the Germans were heard tamping their explosives, and early next morning our camouflet was exploded under theirs, taking them completely by surprise, and effectively concluding hostile mining in this area for a considerable time.

Raids had shown that, on the arrival of the 4th Division, the German front was held by Bavarians, but it was soon noticed that they were replaced by Prussians, and that more guns of all calibres were brought up. At this time our guns were only permitted to fire about four rounds per battery per day, which was a pitiful response to the morning and evening " hates."

On August 23rd, the Battalion went into Brigade reserve at Mailly-Maillet, proceeding a week later to Beaussart in divisional reserve. From the 9th to the 17th September they were in the trenches opposite Beaumont-Hamel, afterwards resting in billets at Varennes. The name of Varennes conjures up in the memory of one officer a picturesque scene. "At the end of the first day," he writes, " the men grouped themselves round the village square with its old church in one corner, and as the brilliant autumn sun slowly sank below the broken line of trees and roof-tops, they commenced to sing, and continued for an hour or more, old Welsh airs and songs in that beautiful untutored harmony of which Welshmen are masters."

The 4th Division held the same sector until the end of the year, the Battalion alternating, with other units, in front line positions at Auchonvillers or opposite Beaumont-Hamel, with rests out of the line at Mailly-Maillet, Varennes or Beaussart. This was an uneventful period ; Beaumont-Hamel had broken many French hopes in earlier months of the war, but it had not yet earned the unenviable reputation in British eyes which it was to gain in 1916. Twice at least in the late autumn of 1915 the Battalion returned from a week's tour of the line without suffering a single casualty, and the records are little more than a diary of work done towards the improvement of the trenches.

The weather from September to December got steadily worse; the front trenches were water-logged, and some of the communication trenches became impassible. Accordingly, when not actively holding the line but in so-called rest, the Battalion was engaged in strengthening the trench system at night, and soon became thoroughly acquainted with such unhealthy spots as Colincamps, the Sucririe, Sunken Road and the Redan. Nevertheless, it was the combined effect of adverse weather and the heavy labour involved in constructing earth and wire defences that told upon the Battalion more than the activities of the enemy.

While at Mailly-Maillet work in the forward areas was done under the guidance of the R.E.'s, and when the numbers of men provided by the companies fell short of those ordered, considerable unpleasantness was occasioned by higher authorities. This difficulty was circumvented by the Sergeant-Major of " C " Company, who adapted the principle of the stage army. The men were counted by the R.E. officer at the entrance to the communication trench, and after going sufficiently far some of them were instructed to climb out and crawl back over the top, to reappear as newcomers. In this way " C " Company could always without difficulty provide parties of any required size!

Mailly-Maillet had been captured from the Germans by the French shortly before the British took over the sector. Positions for heavy guns were being constructed in the orchards, and each battalion quartered there had to find sentry groups. One night the orderly officer visiting sentries found that the group on the Engelbelmur Road had caught a spy dressed in civilian clothes but with a German rifle and bayonet. He had been living in the cellar of a deserted cottage; steps led from the cellar through a trapdoor into the room above, in which were stacks of old furniture. A passage had been made through the furniture to the window and cleverly hidden, and from the window it was only a step to stairs leading from the yard to the first floor, where a window facing the German lines could be used for lamp signalling or for releasing pigeons. As there was no direct evidence of spying he was interned by the French. His bayonet was, however, retained by the orderly officer and is to-day a valued war relic.

Christmas, 1915, was spent at Mailly-Maillet, the men having their dinner at mid-day, and the officers dining together at Headquarters in the evening.

LINES OF COMMUNICATION DUTIES.

Early in January, 1916, the Battalion was withdrawn from the fighting zone for a tour of duty on the Lines of Communications, being again highly commended on their departure by the Generals commanding both the 4th Division and the 12th Brigade for their initiative, efficiency and devotion to duty.

Headquarters and " C " Company went to Etaples, "A" Company to Doullens, " B " to Boulogne and " D " to Calais. Duties consisted principally in guarding ammunition dumps and supply depots, and in finding fatigues for loading and unloading ships and trains. It was a much appreciated rest from the hardships and strain of the trenches.

The following extract from orders of the Inspector General of the Lines of Communication is noteworthy :—" The I.G.C. wishes to express his appreciation of the plucky conduct of No. 3328 Private F. Jones, 1/2nd Monmouthshire Regiment. On the 7th April, 1916, at Calais, Private Jones was crossing a bridge when he heard someone in the water shouting for help. It was dark at the time and the depth of the quayside was at least 12 feet. Private Jones jumped in, caught hold of and supported the man until a rope was thrown to them and both rescued."

Headquarters moved with " C " Company to Boulogne on 10th April, 1916, but no other detachments changed station.

CHAPTER V.

CONVERSION TO PIONEERS—RETURN TO THE SOMME—
" SOMME, 1916 "—INTERLUDE AT YPRES—BACK TO THE SOMME—
LE TRANSLOY—SAILLY-SAILLISEL.

A PIONEER BATTALION.

EIGHTEEN months of trench warfare had brought out the advisability of providing each division with a unit which, while not necessarily possessing the technical qualifications of the Royal Engineers, could efficiently perform their less skilled tasks, and at the same time relieve the fighting troops of much spade work. Accordingly during the winter 1915/16 certain infantry units recruited from mining areas, and therefore specially adept in the use of pick and shovel, were withdrawn from their normal functions and attached to divisions as Pioneer Battalions. The rapidity with which these units could entrench speeded up enormously the consolidation of captured positions, and, being trained and organized as infantry, they were always available as a divisional reserve.

The 2nd Monmouthshires were selected for these duties, and between the 22nd and 27th April, 1916, they received their equipment, the transport alone being nearly doubled to convey the increased number of tools.* They were ordered to join the 29th Division, which, having gained immortal renown at Gallipoli and Suvla, was destined in France to enhance its claims to fame. Its infantry at this time consisted of eleven regular battalions and the Newfoundland Regiment, and the wish expressed by Colonel Roche when the Volunteers parted company with his

---

* It is an odd coincidence that the warrant officer of the R.A.O.C., Conductor N. Honey, who personally issued pioneer stores and equipment to the Battalion in 1916, became its Quartermaster in 1924.

A PIONEER BATTALION

battalion in the South African War " that if ever the Regiment is again called to active service, they will have the assistance of their old comrades of the South Wales Borderers Volunteers " was realized, for the 2nd Monmouthshires found the 2nd South Wales Borderers serving alongside them in the 29th Division.

As pioneers, the 2nd Mons. were no longer called upon for garrison duty in the trenches. Usually they lived in a rearward camp by day, sending working parties forward at night, and occasionally one or two companies were accommodated in reserve positions to facilitate getting to their tasks. Working parties were frequently shelled at work as well as going to and from it, and even when the tired troops got back to camp they were by no means immune from danger, for the enemy's heavy artillery often fired on them, and they were always open to bombing attacks from the air. Throughout their service, however, with the hardest fighting division in France, the 2nd Mons. gained high praise for discipline, ability and steadfastness under the most trying conditions, although their spirit in the nature of their special occupation could not be buoyed up like that of the fighting infantry with the knowledge that sooner or later they would have the chance of " getting a bit of their own back " from the Boche.

In most divisions it was usual for the pioneer battalion to work under the instructions of the C.R.E., doing the less skilled work for the Field Companies. In the 29th Division, however, the Battalion took its instructions from the General Staff, thus working directly under the G.O.C., and so conserving its energies for important tasks. When the Division was relieved from the front line, the Battalion generally continued forward under the orders of Corps Headquarters, and accordingly its periods of rest from the line were few.

When the 29th Division was under orders to attack, its pioneers invariably took a big share in preparation for the offensive and in the consolidation of the ground gained.

Preparation usually took the form of improving the approaches to the assembly position, frequently in digging " kicking-off " trenches to enable the infantry to advance in a line parallel with their objective, and occasionally in repairing roads and clearing obstacles to permit the artillery to move forward.

Consolidation after an attack would entail any of the following main tasks :—(a) digging a new front line, (b) improving and converting a German trench so that fire could be directed to its new front, (c) digging communication trenches across the old No Man's Land, and (d) putting up wire in front of the new line.

Wiring was generally done under the supervision of the R.E.'s, but trench construction was entirely in the hands of the Commanding Officer, once he had had his instructions from the General Staff. Two days or so prior to an attack, the officers of the companies concerned were summoned to Battalion Headquarters, where details of the plans of the infantry were explained, together with the role allotted to the Battalion. If the attack were to be made in daylight, the Pioneers worked after dusk, but in the case of a night assault, they followed the infantry closely and set about the task at once.

If a "kicking-off" line had to be dug, it was usual for two officers of each duty company to reconnoitre the way up to the trenches a day or so before, obtaining from the troops in the line any necessary information and arranging for liaison. On the night when the work was to be done, two officers and a covering party would precede the company by an hour or more and tape out the line of the trench to be dug. The men on their arrival would be set out on their tasks at the appropriate intervals, about five feet, and would start work immediately, platoons leaving independently when they had finished their allotted portions. Work had, of course, to end before daylight, and when further improvements were found necessary the company concerned would rest in dug-outs in the support trenches by day, and proceed again the following night. It was a point of honour among the officers to remain on top and not enter a trench while work was in progress.

RETURN TO THE SOMME.

Having received the bulk of its equipment, the Battalion concentrated at Doullens on 29th April, and reorganized its companies into platoons and sections, most of which had lost their identity during the period on Lines of Communication duties. Route marches were arranged to harden the men, and on the 1st May the Battalion set out by road to join the 29th Division, which was holding the same sector opposite Beaumont-Hamel which the 4th Division was occupying when the Battalion left it in December.

En route they marched past the Corps Commander, Lieutenant-General Sir A. Hunter-Weston, who afterwards spoke to the officers and men in terms of welcome and advice as if they were a Battalion newly arrived from home. During the stand-easy which followed, the information was tactfully conveyed to the General that the Battalion had seen active service in this war before any unit of the 29th Division except one. Sir Aylmer promptly again addressed the men and set the matter right by welcoming " tried troops " to his command.

Soon after resuming the march, the appearance high up in the sky of two hostile obversation balloons signified entrance into the war zone, and companies and platoons opened to wide distances, reaching in this formation their billets at Beaussart.

On entering the 29th Division the Battalion assumed the Divisional badge, a red triangle on each sleeve. It also wore its own mark, a green rectangle with a horizontal strip of red, in the middle of the back below the collar. In addition the men wore the Pioneer's collar badge of crossed pickaxes.

Preparations for the great Somme battle were in full swing, and the 2nd Mons. were put to work at once on making a dry weather track from Acheux to Engelbelmer, which received what in time turned out to be the appropriate name of Rotten Row. They moved on May 5th to a canvas camp at Acheux Wood and on the 10th to another at Mailly Wood, where it was found necessary to dig trenches in which to shelter during periods when the enemy shelled the camp. When the track was completed, they were employed on communication trenches, emplacements for machine guns and trench mortars, and in preparing routes through the trench system for the traffic in guns, ammunition, food and stores which would be required to follow a successful attack. A small detachment sunk a 60-foot well from which excellent, plentiful and much needed water was obtained. During June, Thursdays were devoted to drill and training, a change from the ordinary routine which was much appreciated by the men. On June 17th, the Divisional Commander, Major-General de Lisle, complimented the Battalion on its excellent work, and June 23rd saw it moving its camp, bag and baggage, back to Acheux Wood, where it spent a week of intensive training, during which its share in the coming attack was fully explained.

"SOMME, 1916."

So far as the 2nd Mons. are concerned, the Battle Honour "Somme, 1916" on the Regimental Colour was earned by their presence at the opening of the fight on 1st July, 1916, at Beaumont-Hamel, and at the engagements which resulted in the capture of Le Transloy and Sailly-Saillisel, marking the closing phases of the long-drawn out Somme battle in the early spring of 1917.

The objective allotted to the 29th Division in the opening stage of the Battle of the Somme was Beaumont-Hamel and the German front line system between that village and the River Ancre, the Division being the left of the British attack. The position was of enormous natural strength, the ground rising ridge upon ridge permitting tiers of fire to be poured upon an attack, those behind firing with perfect safety over the heads of those in front. In Beaumont-Hamel itself was a quarry with capacious dug-outs which enabled the enemy to concentrate large numbers of men in absolute security, and available to man within two or three minutes the trench system, no matter how heavily bombarded. Opposite Beaumont-Hamel the lines were some 800 yards apart approaching to about 15 yards at the Redan at the top of the ridge, and again opening to some 600 yards where the Ancre ended them. Thus it will be seen that when the British left their trenches they had wide stretches of ground to cross except at one point, and the Germans had ample time to pour out from their shelters to bring fire to bear. Beaumont-Hamel, which had cost a great many French lives in

"SOMME, 1916"

fruitless assaults in 1914, although since then the sector had been fairly quiet, achieved in the next few weeks an unpleasant notoriety probably third only to Ypres and Verdun.

The attack by the 29th Division on the 1st July failed along its whole front, and consequently the 2nd Monmouthshires, detailed principally for consolidation duties, found other employment. All companies had entered the trench system during the night in fighting order with two day's iron rations, every man with a pick or spade on his back under the equipment and with two sandbags in his belt. Officers were dressed in men's clothing, with rank badges in the shoulder straps, and while it had been possible to issue steel helmets to 200 men, the remainder had to enter action in soft caps, with instructions to replace them with helmets from the dead. Tragic to relate, every man had a steel helmet within a few hours.

The 29th Division experienced for the first time a new form of German barrage, namely, a line of bursting shells extending as far as the eye could see and kept up from zero hour until late in the afternoon. The barrage appeared to consist of a salvo of four shells bursting on the ground about 20 yards apart, followed 30 seconds later by four shrapnel shells exploding in the air. They had scarcely burst before the ground was again rent with high explosives, followed by more shrapnel, and so on.

The attack started at 7.20 a.m., and ten minutes later "A" Company (Major A. H. Edwards, M.C.) moved along Old Beaumont Road to the front line. The Bombing Platoon, led by Lieutenant W. R. Sankey, proceeded up a sunken road to clear the way for three platoons of the company, the first part of whose task it was to carry grenades into Beaumont-Hamel for the use of troops expected to be found there. They were held up by machine-gun fire within a hundred yards of their objective, and with the infantry failure to get on, no further progress was made.

"B" Company (Captain C. Comely) had been detailed to dig communication trenches across No Man's Land. Nos. 5 and 6 Platoons were unable to get to their task because of the trenches being choked by stretcher cases, signallers and orderlies, and they remained in a support trench all day, suffering many casualties from the enemy's shell-fire. Nos. 7 and 8, after great

"SOMME, 1916"

difficulty for the same reason in reaching the front line, made two attempts to get out into No Man's Land to start digging, but as the enemy still held all his positions intact, they were forced back. They commenced sapping forward then, and made a trench which was later of value, enabling withdrawal of the infantry under cover.

Second-Lieutenant L. E. Ford, with a party of 20 men of " B " Company, had for some days previously been engaged in constructing a light railway track from Mailly-Maillet to the front line, with orders to continue to Beaumont-Hamel, immediately it had fallen. Like many others, this plan never materialized.

" C " Company (Captain H. W. E. Bailey) was intended for consolidation work on the third objective when captured, and in consequence of the general failure it did not move.

" D " Company (Captain A. C. Sale) was distributed among the attacking infantry with varying tasks, principally carrying materials for use by consolidating parties.

Sections 1 and 2 of No. 13 Platoon (Lieutenant T. E. R. Williams), laden with stakes and wire, went over the top behind the Lancashire Fusiliers, and turned up Sunken Road, where they were ordered to dump the material and advance over the open. They got within sixty yards of the Germans and, lying under cover of a fold in the ground, dug themselves in. The Fusiliers had been caught by machine-gun fire from every direction, and their remnants were withdrawn when dusk gave its friendly aid. Early in the advance Lieutenant Williams had been severely wounded after crossing the front line trench. Private S. J. Burnett crawled over 100 yards to him under continuous fire, pulled him into a shellhole, and finally brought him back to safety. He undoubtedly rescued his officer at great peril to his own life, an act which was marked by the award to him of the M.M.

Nos. 3 and 4 Sections, advancing with the 16th Middlesex and carrying coils of wire and Bangalore torpedoes, got within biscuit throw of the German line, but had to withdraw with the infantry survivors.

Half of No. 14 Platoon (Second Lieutenant J. E. Simpson) went over with the Royal Fusiliers and shared the same fate, but Nos. 7 and 8 Sections, attached to the Royal Dublin Fusiliers, were ordered into dug-outs when it was found that the enemy's front line remained unshaken. They were later employed in carrying wounded out of the line, returning with ammunition, grenades and rations.

No. 15 Platoon, with Captain Sale in charge, climbed over the top with the Border Regiment, each man carrying eight full water-bottles and some signalling gear. They got well into the middle of No Man's Land before the advance was checked, lying out for over two hours until the Borders were withdrawn. They subsequently busied themselves in getting the wounded away.

No. 16 Platoon (Second Lieutenant H. B. Davies) went over in rear of the K.O.S.B., but when they were held up, joined and assisted " B " Company in their work.

Orders were received in the evening for the Battalion to re-assemble in Mailly Wood, and for small working parties to be detailed to clear the main communication trenches. These parties were found from the reserve of ten per cent. which was always kept back from battle, and companies had all rejoined by midnight.

On July 2nd, the Battalion was placed under orders of the G.O.C. 88th Brigade, to whom Colonel Bowen reported for instructions. In conjunction with an attack on the left by the 4th Division, two battalions of that brigade were to assault at 3 a.m. on the 3rd, supported by the 2nd Mons. If the objective were taken, the Battalion would be employed in consolidating the position, and if not, it would be used in a renewed attack. At 9.30 p.m., companies moved up to their positions in support, being bombarded *en route* with tear-gas shells. Gas goggles were donned, which with the natural darkness made it impossible to see in the trenches. Forward the men struggled, tripping over loose and broken duck-boards, bumping into each other, rifles and feet becoming continually entangled in telephone wires, until it became a veritable nightmare.

"A" and " D " Companies were following behind troops of the 4th Division up a communication trench and were about half-way, when the infantry in front, evidently lost in the darkness, turned about and passed through them, thereby delaying

"SOMME, 1916"

them three hours. " B " and " C " with the Bombers and Lewis Gunners had less bad luck (" C " were actually led over the top through a rain of gas shells) and reached their positions about midnight, only to be informed that the proposed operation was cancelled. The enemy put down his usual heavy artillery fire but the companies got into deep dug-outs and escaped casualties. At 6 a.m. orders to return to Mailly Wood were received, and they were all back two hours later.

No further operations were attempted in this sector by the Division, whose infantry had suffered extremely heavily (one unit lost 90 per cent. of its effectives), compared with which the Battalion had got off very lightly with 11 killed, 106 wounded including 4 officers, and 9 missing.

In addition to Private Burnett, Sergeant J. Jones and Lance-Corporal S. Woodland received Military Medals for their gallantry on the 1st July.

In the days that followed the Battalion accomplished one of its most notable digging exploits. The failure of the attack was attributed to some extent to the infantry having to advance too far exposed to fire, and the 2nd Mons. were therefore ordered to dig a new front line from the Redan to the Ancre closer to the Germans, with communication trenches leading back to the existing front line. Having done this they were to dig another system still more advanced, in fact, within 60 yards of the enemy.

The task was started on the right of the line against the River Ancre. The whole Battalion was out night after night, marching from Mailly Wood in the evening so as to arrive at the front line at dusk. The route led through Engelbelmer and Mesnil-sur-Ancre, the latter village being passed in small parties and at as rapid a rate as possible, because of the heavy shelling to which it was usually subjected. The first night turned out fairly peaceful as the Germans were engaged on repairs to their wire and parapets, but morning showed up the lines of white chalk which the trench-digging men had thrown up, and the enemy lost no time in ranging his guns, trench mortars and machine guns on the work. Every night afterwards the parties were fired at with these weapons persistently, and many casualties occurred.

"SOMME, 1916"

As the work progressed, so longer distances from camp had to be traversed, and a heavy strain, accentuated by the nightly toll of dead and wounded, was imposed on all ranks: that they rose superior to it is evidence of their undaunted spirit.

After the first two nights, during which covering parties were provided by the infantry in the line, the 2nd Mons. found their own protective troops. These parties consisted of a N.C.O. and three or four bombers, stout fellows who lay out in the wet grass all night listening and watching, always the last to come in. They were all volunteers for the job, and it was no uncommon thing for a man to ask his company commander, " Who's covering us to-night, sir ? " and when the well-known names were mentioned, a muttered " Good enough, sir," would indicate that work would proceed as if it were being done miles behind the line, such was the confidence of the men in their comrades. No German patrols ever got through these covering parties.

The trenches were completed about 14th July and the communication trenches a few nights later. It then appeared that the right of the line near the Ancre was still too distant, and the Battalion was turned out for several more nights constructing a fresh and more advanced trench. It was from the system thus dug by the 2nd Mons. that the attack was launched later by the 51st Division which resulted in the capture of Beaumont-Hamel.

On July 18th, the Battalion was inspected by Lieutenant-General Sir A. Hunter-Weston, who complimented it on the amount and quality of the work it had done since it joined the 29th Division, adding in his own inimitable manner that " they might all, when writing home, tell their people that he, their Corps Commander, had told them that they had done their duty and done it well."

The Division was relieved on the 24th, the Battalion handing over its pioneer duties to the 6th South Wales Borderers.

INTERLUDE AT YPRES.

Moving partly by march route and partly by train, the Battalion found itself once more in the Ypres sector, where

INTERLUDE AT YPRES

Headquarters and two companies went to a hutted camp at Brandhoek, while the remainder lived in the cellars of Ypres itself, arriving on July 31st. Here they remained until October 6th.

British and Germans were expending their full energies in the struggle on the Somme, and Ypres for once was a quiet part. The Divisional sector extended from Hooge to Weiltje, and the Battalion was employed principally on trench, road and track improvements, although the first task of the companies quartered in Ypres had been to clean and render gas-proof their own accommodation, and then perform the same work in other cellars, including those of a building believed to have been a reformatory on the Menin Road. As the whole area was under enemy observation, work was generally done at night, but the comparative peacefulness was a welcome rest from the strenuous turmoil of the Somme. Perhaps the most important work was the construction of the communication trench to the front line known as Piccadilly.

The outstanding event was a phosgene gas attack by the Germans on the night of the 8th August, when the bulk of the men were working on Piccadilly Trench. Gas helmets, of the P.H. pattern then in use, were at once put on and in accordance with instructions all ranks stood still until the cloud blew over. The gas was like a white mist, so dense as to make movement over even open ground difficult. It was not followed by an infantry assault, and so well drilled were the men in use of their helmets that only four became casualties.

Major-General de Lisle was always most keen on work in his area, both to improve the defences and to make them generally more habitable, and thoroughly earned the praise of the Army Commander, General Sir H. Plumer, on the improvements effected by the 29th Division during its stay. The 2nd Mons. had been responsible for a great deal of this amid the enormous difficulties inherent to the ground. The soil was water-logged, and a newly dug trench rapidly filled. Breastworks rather than trenches had to be constructed, but a large and successful drainage scheme was carried out by the Battalion which contributed not a little to alleviate conditions over a wide area.

INTERLUDE AT YPRES

Three valued officers were lost during this tour to the Salient. Captains E. Edwards and S. R. Hockaday were badly wounded while directing the work of their companies, and both died soon afterwards. Another company commander, Captain G. E. Foster was wounded and evacuated home, but was able to rejoin in the field a year later.

BACK TO THE SOMME.

The Division was relieved on October 5th, and on the 6th the Battalion followed it once more into the Somme area. In the interval since they were last there the enemy had been forced back a considerable distance, and the Battalion went into camp at Montauban about eight miles in advance of the line held by the British on 1st July. The camp site was found to be a bare patch of ground pitted with shell holes. The Pioneer Battalion Coldstream Guards had spent the morning filling in the worst holes, and they proved helpful friends when tents arrived and had to be pitched. One man who had fallen out on the march to Montauban was picked up and conveyed to camp in a staff car conveying the PRINCE OF WALES.

For a fortnight the Battalion was employed under Corps orders in constructing and repairing roads; it then returned to Divisional control and worked in the trenches. The weather was appalling, so much so in fact that an attack by the Division originally planned for 25th October had, after two postponements, to be abandoned. The Division was relieved on the 30th, and the Battalion again came under Corps control, remaining at Montauban.

It was employed principally in trying to improve the roads from Ginchy to Lesbœufs and Flers, which were in a deplorable condition owing to the heavy rainfall on the shell-softened soil. The first working parties found the corduroy in many places floating in two feet or more of liquid mud, and the whole of this winter was spent in a struggle with mud of the type which is known only to those who served in France and Flanders. It is related that in the closing stages of the Battle of Le Transloy a soldier stuck so deeply in the mud close to the firing line that he could only be extricated before dawn—then rapidly approaching —by undoing his braces and pulling him bodily out of his trousers and gum-boots.

While at work the areas were spasmodically shelled, especially on the few fine days which made aerial observation possible. Several times too, hostile aeroplanes made unwelcome visits to the camp, dropping bombs and firing machine guns. On October 23rd, for instance, a German aeroplane flew over the camp in the early morning. He dropped a bomb near the M.O.'s tent, killing one man and wounded several, amongst others Captain J. Sainsbury, R.A.M.C., who had been attached to the battalion for over a year. He was a most popular M.O., and his immaculate dress and cheery smile will be remembered by all who knew him.

Again, on 23rd November, an enemy naval gun, quickly christened "Whistling Percy," shelled the camp all morning. Many lives must have been lost but for the state of the ground, which was practically a quagmire, into which the delayed fuse shells penetrated deeply before exploding. Only one man was wounded but "A" Company officers had a marvellous escape, for their mess hut received a direct hit while they were inside. Lieutenant Haggis was at the time counting the canteen takings, and the table was covered with French paper money. Fortunately the shell was a "dud," the only casualty being a mascot puppy, "Blighty," and all the money was subsequently recovered, although some notes had been buried deep below the surface of the ground. Two nights later, to the regret deep of all ranks, Captain C. W. Taunton, one of the few officers left who went out with the Battalion in 1914, was killed by a direct hit on his tent.

On 18th November, the Division occupied the Lesbœufs–Le Transloy trenches and the 2nd Mons. took over the pioneer duties of the sector, but without changing camp. Most of the work was performed at night, but parties were also employed by day on duties which would not disclose their presence, such as laying duck-boards.

The work which engaged the Battalion was the construction of long communication trenches, first Flers Alley and then

BACK TO THE SOMME

Flank Avenue. Owing to the weather the work was heartbreaking, for a length of trench dug and revetted one night would be found on the next to contain anything from one foot to two feet of muddy water. This would wash away the sides and undo the work of the best revetting, causing further falls and stoppages. At night everyone preferred the risk of being hit going over the top to that of being stuck in the mud. But on one occasion, just before the Division went out to rest, word was received that the G.O.C. would visit the front line next day and wished to reach the front line " dry shod and in comparative safety." Who was responsible for the wording of these instructions was not known, but it was hoped that he appreciated the efforts of the Battalion that night on the worst 300 yards of the trench. At all events the General did not reach the front line dry shod.

Until December 18th, the Division being in Corps reserve, the Battalion was employed on laying the bed for a Decauville railway line between Montauban and Combles. An extract from a diary for December 13th reads : " The supervising R.E. officer expressed his satisfaction with the work being done, which was performed under difficulties, yesterday's snow having turned to rain, the earth being consequently reduced to a semiliquid state by no means ideal for the building of the bed of a railway line."

Rumours had been prevalent for some time, but not generally trusted, of a rest away from the effect if not the sound of guns. Their confirmation about the middle of December was received with general satisfaction, for with the exception of the move from Mailly to Ypres at the end of July, the Battalion had been working practically without cessation and always within reach of the guns since the end of April, and was badly in need of a rest. The period since their return to the Somme had been very trying for all ranks, and although battle casualties were not heavy, many officers and men were incapacitated by illness due to the terribly wet conditions and the long marches to and from their nightly tasks. There were always sufficient officers to arrange for half their number to rest from work, but there never had been sufficient men to allow of any relief without danger of the work falling behind. The men at this time were more worn than at any other period of the war, before or subsequently. Many of those who were not officially " sick " were in a very run-down state, with a high pulse rate and low temperature. These symptoms of exhaustion were the result of months of unceasing work in inclement weather, in the constant presence of death or ghastly wounds.

On 19th December, therefore, a war-worn Battalion entrained at Trones Wood for Ville-sur-Somme. The day was bitterly cold, and when billets were reached a few cases of frost-bitten feet were reported. The following day the journey was continued by rail to Foudrinoy, where a stay of three weeks was made, during which the change to good food and regular hours, and the respite from mental tension, worked wonders on the health and spirit of all ranks.

On Christmas Day, Colonel Bowen entertained the officers to dinner at the Chateau where his headquarters were established, and after " Crawshay Bailey," and other regimental choruses, they adjourned to a concert arranged in the Sergeants' Mess.

Training was carried out daily, principally on " the company in attack " with some weapon training and ceremonial drill. General de Lisle inspected the Battalion on 9th January, 1917, and stated that " everything was as it should be, and he was proud to have them in his Division."

Good times had a habit in France of coming to an end all too soon, and on January 12th the Battalion started back for the line, spending one day in a train and the second in marching to Maricourt. On the 14th, Headquarters and " C " Company were once more at Montauban, while the other three companies were at the Hogsback and Morval. Once more the daily round of track laying and trench improvement, with its steady toll of casualties, commenced. One such casualty, specially recorded in a diary which usually only noted numbers killed and wounded, marked the passing of a good soldier, and is repeated here in his memory. The entry reads : " 17-1-17. Casualties : O.R. Killed 1—No 1877 Pte Cawsey W., " C " Coy., a battalion runner, one of the most cheerful and most courageous soldiers in the Battalion, and his death is very much regretted by everybody."

This tour in the trenches was intensely cold, fuel was scarce and snow lay on the ground for several weeks. It was a relief from the wet and mud of previous tours, however, and rumours of an attack began to create excitement.

About this time, the powers that were developed a passion for the salvage of material lying on the battlefield, and working parties were always expected to bring back anything found, no matter in how damaged a state it might appear. Colonel Bowen tried to imbue all under him with a salvage complex by setting a personal example (a quality which was one of the greatest factors for the success of his command). During his nightly trips of inspection he was wont to wander about the open, visiting all companies in turn, and would be certain to find some derelict tools, bits of equipment and so on lying about. These he would collect and hand over to the first party he came across, and woe betide the luckless subaltern who was unable to account for them next day! One night his figure loomed through the darkness, laden with half a dozen assorted rifles and an odd pick or two, and approached a party working in a trench, from the depths of which came a disconsolate groan: " 'Ere comes the blinkin' arsenal!"

LE TRANSLOY.

During the recent rest the 87th Brigade had undergone special preparatory training, for the 29th Division was not one to rest content with its failure of the 1st of July, or the disappointments of the cancelled attacks of October. It had been decided to mark the Kaiser's approaching birthday by attacking his troops at Le Transloy, and everyone was in the highest spirits.

The normal works programme of the Pioneers was suspended without warning on 20th January, and one hundred men from each company were sent up at night to dig a new trench from which the attack was to be launched. The trench was 640 yards long, but before dawn it had been completed along its whole length and provided with fire-steps. Next day Colonel Bowen received the following message from Lieutenant-

LE TRANSLOY

Colonel G. G. Fuller, Chief of the Divisional Staff :—" The G.O.C. wishes you to convey to the troops who took part in digging the front line trench last night his appreciation of their excellent work. The performance was all the more creditable since little time was allowed for organizing the working parties."

Lieutenant H. Ll. Hughes writes racily of this task : " It proved a most amusing affair. All four companies turned out and, I believe, the three R.E. Field Companies with working parties of infantry. It was a bright moonlight night, and the snow which had been lying for several days was frozen hard, making the surface treacherous and slippery. We arrived on the scene first and got to work, and then in the distance heard the other parties coming, making a fearsome noise. They came apparently prepared to stay a week, with mess-tins, shovels, picks, rifles and accoutrements galore, and as every other man appeared to slip on the ice and crash heavily and noisily, the din must have been heard in Germany. The Boche was too wise to get really nasty,—at least he contented himself with a little machine-gun fire and a lovely display of Verey lights,— and the work was peaceably finished."

The attack on Le Transloy was made on January 27th, the barrage opening at 5.30 a.m., and soon after that hour " C " Company in Hogsback Trench saw prisoners coming down. Many had their blankets neatly rolled and strapped to their packs, and one carried a canary in a cage. Their uniforms were spotless, and it transpired that they had been caught in the middle of a relief.

The Battalion was called upon to dig, after dusk, two communication trenches to connect the old front line with the captured position. " B " Company (Captain A. L. Coppock) was detailed to work on the right trench and " C " Company (Captain J. T. George) that on the left.

" B " Company reached the old front line about 8 p.m., but found the troops there uncertain of the situation. A covering party of six bombers, under Sergeant A. Hodges, was sent forward and was almost immediately fired on, the sergeant and one of the men being hit. A second party went out and ascertained that the enemy was still in possession of the very point at which the communication trench was ordered to enter the

German line. The enemy evidently had fixed rifles bearing on the spot where the men clambered out, for although it was dark, several were hit. Captain Coppock, leaving the company in charge of Lieutenant R. T. Saunders, went back to the headquarters of the battalion in the line for information and instructions, and during his absence Colonel Bowen appeared on the scene at about 11.30 p.m. On the situation being explained, he at once climbed over the top with Second Lieutenant M. T. Howells, and found his way, revolver in hand, to a post of the 2nd South Wales Borderers in the captured trench. From there he taped a line back about 30 degrees from the original direction, and the company commenced work about midnight, arrangements having been made with the S.W.B. for their protection. During all this time shells and bullets had been flying, and " B " Company suffered a number of casualties while waiting to start work. Owing to the new line of trench being longer than that for which numbers had been estimated, reinforcements from " D " Company, waiting in the support line, had to be called up. With their assistance, despite the hardness of the frozen ground and the harrassing hail of bullets and shells, the trench was dug through by 4.30 a.m. to an average depth of four feet, and a strong post had been constructed in the centre. This success was largely due to the Colonel's determination to see a difficult job through, to his complete disregard of personal danger, and to the energy which his strong personality radiated.

" C " Company also reached the old front line about 8 p.m. Captain George had gone on ahead to tape out the trench and Lieutenants F. L. Spencer and H. Ll. Hughes followed with the company, together with Lieutenant H. T. Nelmes and his platoon of " D " Company. The men had been given their tasks along the tape and had been digging for about ten minutes when the Germans put down a heavy barrage upon them. In spite of the frozen state of the soil the older men had already got into it and made cover about a foot deep. Unfortunately, a draft of inexperienced men had recently joined the Battalion; they knew little about digging and had barely removed the snow from the surface when the barrage fell and so had no cover. The shelling continued for about twenty minutes, and they suffered several casualties. Prominent among the stretcher-bearers, for whom there were many calls, was Lance-Corporal Jones, of Little Mill, one of the bravest and most devoted of that hardworked band. In running to a wounded man he was hit and, to the deep regret of all ranks, killed with four others.

"A few moments after the bombardment began," writes Lieutenant Hughes, " Captain George came dashing over the top, crouching and leaping from shell-hole to shell-hole. He was dressed in a funny short leather coat he had bought in Amiens, and as he ran he shouted ' Tripe ! Tripe ! Tripe ! ' I feared the worst had happened to him, but I learned later that the code word asking for artillery retaliation that night was ' Tripe,' and he was rushing back through the bombardment to get to the telephone in a forward post to send the message. In this he was successful. Soon afterwards the shelling died down, and the work proceeded. Colonel Bowen, who had been with " B " Company, had seen our plight, and came over fearing we had been wiped out. He was relieved to find the company still working on the trench, which was dug to a depth of six feet before we left."

" B " Company's casualties were ten men killed and seven wounded, " C " Company's being four killed and eight, including one officer, wounded.

The outstanding feature of this operation was that the ground was solidly frozen, a condition which would have baffled men less used to handling a pick on hard surfaces. " The Story of the 29th Division " observes :—" The consolidation of the captured ground by the 2nd Monmouthshire Pioneers under Lieutenant-Colonel Bowen's personal supervision was a remarkable feat. The ground was frozen to a depth of eighteen inches and of course as hard as iron. Yet the line was dug in twenty minutes in the face of hostile fire at close range."

Several Military Medals were won that night for deeds which were typical of many others which have gone unmarked. The following deeds for which some of the medals were awarded are given to illustrate the conditions of the night :—

Sergeant C. Griffith was acting as Platoon Commander and by his devotion to duty and courage kept his men in good spirits in spite of considerable casualties due to heavy shelling. He set an excellent example which was of the greatest assistance to his Company Commander.

LE TRANSLOY

Lance-Corporal T. Rose, when in in intense bombardment a direct hit buried several men, at once got hold of a small party, and by his energy and coolness got them quickly to work, rescuing two of those who had been buried but were still alive. Later in the evening he was particularly conspicuous by his coolness in carrying on his work, his good example being of great assistance in keeping his comrades steady.

Private J. Lewis was wounded during the bombardment, but after being bandaged he requested permission to go on with his work, and he accordingly finished his task in spite of his wound. The loss of a man would have meant a piece of trench not being dug through, and it was due to Lewis's determination that his section's particular bit was completed.

The Battalion received special mention in despatches and in the official communique to the press for its work at Le Transloy. General de Lisle called personally on the Commanding Officer to express his pleasure, and the Corps Commander, Lord Cavan, wrote congratulating Colonel Bowen on the work done, stating that the spirit and determination shown by all ranks was worthy of the highest tradition. For their gallantry and leadership, Colonel Bowen was awarded a bar to his D.S.O., and Captain George received the M.C.

That appreciation of the work of the Battalion was not confined to the higher ranks alone is evidenced by General de Lisle, who relates that he asked an infantry sergeant what impressed him most during the Le Transloy action. The reply was: "The wonderful accuracy of our artillery and the remarkable bravery of Colonel Bowen and his Pioneers."

SAILLY-SAILLISEL.

On February 9th the Division was relieved, the 2nd Mons. moving to Meaulte, where training was undergone amid comparatively peaceful surroundings. Here on the 15th the Battalion enjoyed a variety concert by talented performers from its own ranks, got together by Lieutenant Baddeley.

SAILLY-SAILLISEL

The Battalion marched to Hardecourt Camp on the 19th February, the Division taking over the Sailly-Saillisel sector two days later. The long frost which had bound the country since the beginning of January, had broken and the soil was rapidly reverting to its accustomed muddy state. A day later Headquarters and " B " Company moved to Wedgewood Camp, while the other companies went forward to Fregicourt and Combles. Until the 28th the companies were employed in building trench-mortar emplacements, and improving and draining the trenches. An important task, the rapid conclusion of which brought a telephoned message of appreciation from Corps Headquarters, was the digging and filling in, in four days, of 1,060 yards of cable trench, six feet deep.

An attack on Sailly-Saillisel was launched by the 86th Brigade early on the 28th February, and in the afternoon the Staff Captain warned Colonel Bowen over the telephone that the Battalion might be required to take over the captured line during the night. Preparations were at once made, but later it was found that the infantry were quite capable of coping with the enemy's counter-attacks. After dark "A" Company (Captain W. D. Howick) was ordered forward to dig a communication trench across the old No Man's Land, while " B " Company (Captain A. L. Coppock) was placed at the disposal of the Officer Commanding 2nd Royal Fusiliers.

"A" Company came under heavy shell-fire twenty minutes after starting, but got through with only three men wounded. Captain Howick went across to the captured position, Potsdam Trench, and placed out a covering party of bombers. He then taped a line back, got his men out and by 1.30 a.m. they had completed their task.

" B " Company were caught in the same heavy shelling, but by taking cover in shell-holes they escaped without casualties. As they were passing through Sailly-Saillisel, however, a heavy shell concentration fell on them, and they lost several killed and wounded. Captain Coppock reported to the Royal Fusiliers about 8.30 p.m. and was ordered to dig a communication trench across to Pfalz Trench. Unlike the Le Transloy digging, the difficulty this night was in the muddiness of the soil. Reinforcements from " C " Company had to be sent for, and even so the trench was not completed until nearly dawn.

Two platoons of "A" Company and one of " C " were retained to garrison posts in the old British line. " C " Company's platoon found that its allotted trench had been obliterated by shell-fire, and was thereupon sent to garrison Sailly and Cushy strong-posts. On the following night these posts were relieved, and "A" Company was employed in clearing Potsdam Trench and providing it with firesteps. Parts of the trench were flooded, others had been completely blown in, but the company cleared a hundred yards of it during the night.

On the night of the 2nd/3rd March, " B " Company had to dig a trench for the flank defence of the new position, and, although the length was double what had been anticipated, the men put their backs into it and, not being over-hampered by hostile fire, completed the task by 3 a.m.

While " B " Company was thus employed, " C " Company (Captain J. T. George, M.C.) was ordered to dig a new traversed trench in advance of the front line and about 60 yards from the German trenches. Captain (then Lieutenant) R. T. Saunders writes :—" Captain George and myself were the officers accompanying " C " Company, and we set out from the dug-outs at Combles, arriving about 7 p.m. at a quarry where advanced Brigade Headquarters were. Here we were met by Colonel Bowen who had been in consultation with the Brigadier, and final orders were issued. The Colonel decided to go ahead with George to tape out the work : I was to bring the men along in an hour's time. Colonel Bowen seemed to have a premonition that he would not get through that night, for he said to me : ' Well, Saunders, I'm afraid its going to be a sticky night, so I will write out detailed orders for you.' He wrote out the order which follows with his accustomed clarity, and then he left with George and a small covering party.

" O.C. ' C ' Coy.

1. Your Coy. with 15 men of B Coy. will continue the work done last night on Potsdam by digging a traversed trench N.W. to U 8 d $2\frac{1}{2}$-$5\frac{1}{2}$ from U 8 d $3\frac{1}{2}$-4, that is : the left of A Coy's work last night as shown on the attached sketch.

2. Dimensions 5' deep, 4' wide at top, 3' wide at bottom. The bays are to be firestepped.

3. Care must be taken that the enemy do not surprise the party working.

4. The sandbags carried up are to be handed to the NFLDS at the junction of the right C.T. with Potsdam Trench.

2.3.17
7.30 p.m.   A. J. H. Bowen, Lt-Col.

5. Leave work report and sketch of trench dug at Bde. HQ for me.   A.J.H.B.

"About 8 p.m.," Captain Saunders continues, " I led the company up and, finding no guide awaiting me, I went along the front line where I met a Newfoundland officer, who told me that Colonel Bowen had been killed and Captain George wounded. I went forward to the covering party and withdrew them, not finding any tape. After consultation with the Newfoundland officer, I set the men to work in the front line and proceeded to the headquarters of his battalion. Here I found George, who had been blown up by a shell. Despite the fact that he was badly shaken, he gave me the exact location of Colonel Bowen's body and details of what had happened. I returned to the company, found the Colonel, and had his body carried down. He had been shot through the left arm, the bullet penetrating his heart."

Thus passed a man who had made a proud name for his battalion in a division justly famed for fine soldiers. Originally a member of the 4th Volunteer Battalion The South Wales Borderers, he came to the 2nd Monmouthshires on the formation of the Territorial Force in 1908. He commanded a company when the Battalion landed in France in 1914 and throughout his whole service had inspired all under him with his spirit of keenness and self-sacrifice. He was a detached and rather silent man, gifted with enormous determination, and his constant study and mastery of minute detail led to the smooth running of the battalion machine on lines as precise as the rapid changes of war would permit. Unsparing of his subordinates when occasion demanded, he was least sparing of himself. Fearless

Colonel JOHN EVANS, D.S.O., T.D., D.L.
Commanding Officer 1917 - 1923.

of danger and untiring in energy, he had a way of appearing where shells and bullets were thickest and where difficulties abounded, with no thought but to get the best out of his men for the greater good of their comrades of the Division. His presence alone seemed to dissipate difficulties. Those who served with him knew that his influence remained with the Battalion long after his death. His epitaph in "The Story of the 29th Division" is: "He was not a regular soldier, but so completely a soldier by temperament and self-culture that he was indistinguishable from the very finest type the British Army can produce. The G.O.C. was not exaggerating when he said that Bowen's death was a loss to the whole army."

Corps orders of the 7th of March, referring to Sailly-Saillisel, said:—"The Corps Commander considers the work done extremely satisfactory, as also the wiring of the captured trenches. The very greatest credit is due to the Monmouths. The loss of their gallant Colonel is deplored by the whole Corps."

His body was laid to rest in the military cemetery at Combles on the 3rd March in the presence of as many as could attend at such short notice.

The Division was relieved on the 4th March and the Battalion went into billets at Meaulte. Major J. Evans, who had been detached in charge of the Divisional Works Battalion, rejoined to take command, and was duly promoted. He had served many years with the Battalion before the war, and had been in France with it for the previous twelve months.

Intensive training was the order of the day at Meaulte, and while the 2nd Mons. practised "fighting in open warfare" their special function as pioneers was not neglected. On one occasion interesting experiments in rapid digging were made in the presence of the Divisional Commander. Three methods were tried, some of the men working with equipment and others without it. The "intensive" method consisted in one man working for two minutes on three yards of trench, then, having two reliefs, resting for four minutes, while his reliefs in turn took on the task; the "semi-intensive" comprised three men on two men's tasks, thus giving ten minutes' work and five minutes' rest; while the "ordinary" method was the allotment of lengths of five feet per man, each of whom worked and rested in his own time. The conclusion reached was that the "ordinary" method obtained the best results.

But "resting" from the line was not all work, and among sports events, the 88th Brigade organized a football competition for all companies in Meaulte. "C" Company reached the final round with a company of the 4th Worcesters, and after a very exciting game, including an extra half-hour, the match was left drawn, each side having scored one goal. On the replay, two days later, "C" Company won by two goals to nil, gaining a handsome silver cup, presented by the Y.M.C.A., which was handed to the captain, Lieutenant R. T. Saunders, by the Corps Commander, Lord Cavan.

On March 20th, the Division moved back to the Cavillon area, the Battalion finding itself in its old billets at Foudrinoy. Here drafts were absorbed and training of all kinds, including rapid entrenching, was carried out. Here also was encountered a French farmer, who put in a large claim for compensation for a pear tree, said to have been demolished for firewood by a man of "C" Company. When the most likely culprit was interrogated by his platoon commander, he, of course, "knew nothing about it," although he added as an afterthought: "Don't you pay, sir; it was all rotten and wouldn't burn and wasn't worth anything."

CHAPTER VI.

"SCARPE, 1917"—"YPRES, 1917"—"PILCKEM"—
"LANGEMARCK, 1917"—"POELCAPELLE"—"CAMBRAI, 1917."

THE FIRST BATTLE OF THE SCARPE.

ON March 30th, the Division commenced trekking north and after a march by easy stages with occasionally a halt of a day or two, the Battalion entered Arras on Easter Sunday, April 8th, behind the area from which on the following day the British Third Army was to commence the First Battle of the Scarpe. It was getting dark as the companies were led off to their billets by guides of the advance party, and guns and howitzers were firing from nearly every garden and street corner in the last stages of the preliminary bombardment. The noise reverberating among the buildings was ear-shattering; and it seemed strange to find in this big town, mainly in ruins as it was, a shop here and there still open and showing a brave window display of Easter novelties.

The attack opened at dawn on April 9th and made considerable progress. The Battalion was employed during the day, two companies working at a time, in clearing and repairing the Arras-Cambrai road where the opposing trench systems had crossed it. Owing to the heavy shelling work could not start before noon, but after that hour the capture or retirement of German guns permitted almost unimpeded progress. When the first filling in and levelling of the trenches had been completed, and the passage of horse-drawn traffic rendered possible, the soft parts of the road, where shell-holes and trenches had been, were made good with sleepers. The laying of these was no easy matter, as traffic was continually passing and the road was very congested, there being two lines of traffic forward and one trying to come back. At regular intervals the Germans sent over armour piercing shells from a long range: the gun

THE FIRST BATTLE OF THE SCARPE

could be heard before the shells arrived. Fortunately, most of them landed in the soft ground beside the road and only splashed the parties with mud. By 4 a.m. on the 10th the road was fit for lorries, and as soon as the last obstruction was cleared a heavy flow of traffic—guns, ammunition lorries, supply wagons and staff cars—passed in a steady stream. Snow fell heavily during the late afternoon of the 9th, but so inspiring a sight was the arrival of armoured cars and cavalry that some of the 2nd Mons. dreamed that night of open warfare, the enemy on the run, and even of peace. Large batches of prisoners had come along the road through the working parties, escorted usually by slightly wounded men, but many came in alone, enquiring the way. Everything pointed to a big victory.

The rest of the week was spent in making good the Arras-Tilloy road. The work was done during the day and at high pressure to allow the artillery to move forward. Whilst the enemy was fairly quiet for the first two days, the conditions under which the Battalion worked for the latter part of the week were anything but comfortable, as each night new batteries moved into position where the work of the day had ended, the result being that on the following morning the Germans searched all round the parties with shell-fire to try to locate the guns. Much valuable work was done, too, in salvaging and setting on their way the many tanks which had stuck in the wide, deep trenches they had had to negotiate on the first day.

On April 13th, the 29th Division took over the line about Monchy le Preux, and on the 16th "C" and "D" Companies were detailed to dig a defence line round the east edge of that village. After dusk the two company commanders were conducted through the village, which at the time was being shot to pieces, to the site of the task, where they proceeded to mark out with tape the line of the required trench. Just as they completed the taping the companies arrived, preceded by a string of mules, which traversed a good length of the tape before they could be induced to move off it. A pack mule under ordinary conditions is not easily persuaded, and under shell-fire its stubbornness baffles description, although it is understood that the company commanders concerned essayed the impossible with most of the language in their vocabulary.

THE FIRST BATTLE OF THE SCARPE

The companies were accommodated in a trench which in the attack had been named the Brown Line. It was in very poor condition, and although the Pioneers had a reputation for making any trench habitable and reasonably comfortable within a few hours, the Brown Line defeated their efforts. There were no materials available for its repair, and the rain of the first night was incessant. To add to the discomfort, a battery of field guns was in position close behind it, attracting a great deal of enemy fire to the vicinity. On the 18th they exchanged duties with "A" and "B" Companies who had been engaged on the rearward roads, but on the 19th the work was completed and the Battalion concentrated again at Arras, very relieved to get away at last from the continuous shelling to which the men had been subjected.

THE SECOND BATTLE OF THE SCARPE.

The Second Battle of the Scarpe started on April 23rd. While " C " and " D " Companies remained on road work, "A" and " B " were detailed to dig communication trenches across to the new positions. Both companies moved off from their billets at 6.30 p.m., and proceeded to the Monchy Inner Defence Line where they expected to be met by their respective commanders, who had gone ahead as usual to reconnoitre.

Captain W. D. Howick, of "A" Company, had been told at the 88th Brigade Headquarters that it was impossible for him to work on the line laid down in operation orders as the enemy had not been driven out of his position, and that instead he was to work under orders of the Worcestershire Regiment. This unit was on the right of the Division, and as the troops further to the right had failed to reach their objectives, their position was by no means secure, nor was communication easy.

The shelling was intense and Captain Howick was unable for a time to get to the rendezvous with his company, nor were the platoons able to communicate with each other. One platoon commander, Lieutenant R. G. Noble, gives the following account of the night's experiences :—" I had sent out a couple of runners to try to get orders, but these not returning I sent my sergeant —an Ebbw Vale man whose name I cannot recall—with a companion. Not even these returned, and as the shelling was the heaviest I had ever been through, I was afraid they had all been killed. I did not like ordering any more to go out, so went myself, leaving a corporal in charge. A stretcher bearer came voluntarily with me, and we worked our way forward, eventually getting near one of the tanks stranded in the first attack. Hearing someone calling, we moved over and found Colonel Evans and Major Comely. They had just arrived, and were overjoyed to see us and to know that my platoon at least was intact. This was quite the worst night for shelling I ever put in, and I went through a lot." The shelling slackened after a time, and "A" Company were enabled to get to work about midnight in the line held by the Worcesters. They left off about 2.30 a.m., having improved some hundred yards of the position.

"B" Company had less difficulty and their commander having been able to tape out a line, they finished their allotted task in good time. They were unfortunate, however, in that two heavy shells, falling in the trench where they waited before commencing work, killed twelve of their number, including Second Lieutenant R. A. Cruickshank, and severely wounded five others.

On the 27th the Battalion marched to Gouy, the Division having been relieved, and on the following day further back to Couin, but returned to Arras on 2nd May. During this brief rest a letter was received by Colonel Evans from the Chief Engineer, XVIII. Corps, thanking him, his officers and men for the "really good work they have performed since the battle of the 9th April. I have not yet met officers and men who have tried harder to carry out their instructions, and I consider the work they accomplished on the Tilloy-Wancourt road as very fine."

Until 14th May the 2nd Mons. were again under this Corps for road work, but it spent the second half of the month further forward, the Division being once more in the line. An attack on Infantry Hill was made on the 19th, and the Battalion stood by for consolidation duties, but the assault failed. On the 30th

THE SECOND BATTLE OF THE SCARPE

a renewed attack resulted in a breach in the enemy's lines, and " C " Company who had gone to Shrapnel Trench to be near the scene of the operations had a most unpleasant night.

The attack was timed for 11.30 p.m., but ten minutes before zero hour the enemy placed a heavy and accurate artillery and machine-gun barrage on our lines. At 12.30 a.m. word was received that the position was believed to have been taken, and " C " Company went forward under fire which had not slackened in the least and through a trench knee-deep in mud. The enemy position was found to have been captured, and then abandoned because it was full of water and was badly enfiladed by hostile machine guns. The company thereupon returned to Tilloy. It had been under severe shell-fire throughout the night, had lost 25 killed (including Second Lieutenant A. King) and wounded, had a large number of men shaken and bruised, had sloughed through miles of mud, and had nothing in the end to show for it.

The forward companies returned on June 1st to Arras, and on the 5th the Battalion marched to Le Meillard for a rest which lasted twelve days. The officers have grateful memories of this delightful Picardy village and of the charming hospitality of a French lady who arranged tennis parties and vied with the other inhabitants in trying to remove painful thoughts of recent experiences. The Battalion combined with the Field Ambulance while billeted here in holding sports, at which " D " Company carried off most of the honours.

THE BATTLE OF YPRES, 1917.

" By universal consent," says the 29th Divisional historian, " the Third Battle of Ypres represents the utmost that war has so far achieved in the way of horrors. What the future holds it is idle to imagine. But the cramped theatre with its slimy canals, becks, sloughs, bogs and inundations, its shelled duckboard tracks, its isolated outposts, its incessant shelling and incessant rain, its mists and fogs, its corpses and its pestilential, miasmic odours outdid anything that the Somme or Arras could boast, and it dragged on from the 31st July till the 10th November, 1917. The craters were more numerous and mud was deeper. There was also the added horror of mustard gas, which could cling about a dug-out for days in spite of fires."

Under such conditions the Battalion existed for five months, seldom out of range of the enemy's artillery, for even when the Division was relieved from time to time in the line, its Pioneers remained behind to assist other divisions, or at best had a very brief rest.

From its pleasant billets at Le Meillard the Battalion travelled by rail on June 17th to Proven, whence it marched to Ondbank in the Belgian Army's area. Preparations were being made for a renewal of the British offensive which had begun ten days earlier with the capture of the Messines Ridge, and until the 29th Division arrived on the 25th, the Battalion was employed under the 38th (Welsh) Division in repairing roads and making tracks. On June 27th it moved to dug-outs on the canal bank near Essex Farm, the same area in which it had fought in April and May of 1915, and in which it came across the graves of many old Monmouthshire comrades.

Here it was employed in constructing the Bard and Marengo causeways over the Yser Canal. This work was in full observation of hostile balloons, and fire was directed so accurately each day that the work was destroyed almost as fast as it was done until Captain R. B. Comely, who was commanding " C " Company at Bard Causeway, adapted the principles of camouflage. He noted carefully the positions of the shell-holes on the causeway and, having filled them at night and laid beech planks on top, he caused buckets of mud from the canal to be spread in circles on the planks. The German observers thought evidently that the work had been given up, for no further shells disturbed it, and guns crossed it soon after zero hour on the day of attack.

" D " Company, under Captain M. F. Turner, was detached during this period for work with a Yorkshire pioneer battalion on railway construction. Their duties took them well forward and they suffered comparatively heavy casualties.

Sergeant J. Hale of " C " Company received the M.M. for displaying conspicuous bravery one day when a party under him was caught in an artillery barrage, and Captain R. B. Comely was awarded a bar to his M.C., and Company-Sergeant-Major T. Johnson the D.C.M., for their courage and leadership during these days.

Work under constant shell-fire had caused the Battalion many losses, and it was glad to move out to Caribou Camp, near Proven, on July 20th, for a much needed rest. While here it secured the largest number of wins in the Divisional Boxing Tournament, and here also Major-General de Lisle presented it with a post-horn to mark his appreciation of efforts to maintain a battalion band.

" PILCKEM."

The 2nd Mons. returned to the forward area on July 29th in readiness for the Third Battle of Ypres, which opened on the 31st. The 29th Division did not take part in this, the first stage of this long operation, but the Battalion was attached to the Guards Division, who were in the Boisinghe area with French troops on their left.

A few days before, it had been reported that the enemy had evacuated his front trenches. Reconnoitring patrols confirmed this and the allies were thus able to establish posts across the Canal before the battle opened. Zero was at 3.50 a.m., and the attack moved successfully over the crest of the Pilckem Ridge, although at many points German machine-gunners in their concrete " pill-boxes " delayed the advance, until one after another they were overcome.

"A" and "B" Companies followed as soon as the Ridge was captured and began to clear the road through Pilckem to Iron Cross. They were relieved by " C " and " D " Companies at 2 p.m., by which time the Germans having recovered from the shock of the attack were bombarding the road heavily. Sergeant Powell, who had won the M.M. at Le Transloy, fell wounded and with Pickford, a stretcher-bearer who went to his assistance, was killed when a second shell fell close. It miraculously left Captain Comely untouched, for he too was attending to Powell at the time.

"PILCKEM"

Work on the roads and light railways continued until the 29th relieved the Guards Division on August 8th, taking over the line between Langemarck and Wijdendrift on the Steenbeck. The Steenbeck was shown on the maps as a stream ten feet wide, but shelling had destroyed its banks and dammed its flow, causing the water to spread over a strip of country half a mile wide, thereby turning it into an impassable morass. Over this, after the capture of Langemarck, the Battalion made duck-board tracks, two boards wide supported on piles driven deep into the mud. Sad was the fate of any man who slipped from these boards when no comrade was near to pull him back to safety!

"LANGEMARCK."

On August 16th, the Division participated in a further attack by the British Fifth Army and, advancing east of the village of Langemarck, reached their objective, the line of the Broembeck stream. Two platoons of "A" Company, under Second Lieutenant H. J. Hopkins, went over with the attacking troops, taking tapes to mark out a way through the swamps, so that reinforcing or relieving parties could find their route quickly.

On the 28th the Division was relieved by the Guards and spent September out of the line, but the 2nd Mons. remained forward, maintaining and extending the duck-board tracks and performing defensive work such as wiring the Wijdendrift road.

"BROODSEINDE."

In the week following, the Battalion was engaged in constructing a light railway track leading to the forward gun positions, which were only some 400 yards behind the front line, although concealed from the enemy by a slight rise in the ground. Work was carried out at night, the parties starting in daylight, then marching some five or six miles, and leaving the task when it was light enough for hostile balloons to observe them; in fact, if they were late in departing they were invariably shelled off. On one or two occasions the men were fortunate in getting lifts back to camp on empty ammunition trucks hauled by motor engines, thus escaping the discomfort of marching on the roads which were a seething mass of lorries and men, one line struggling up and the other down in the darkness. Two soldiers of another unit were encountered one night walking from the front arm in arm in a most reckless manner, only avoiding the crawling lorries as if by the help of Providence. From their gait they appeared to be drunk, but when spoken to it was found that both had been blinded by enemy gas, and were endeavouring to find their way to a dressing station. Needless to say, a guide was immediately provided.

Companies when not turned out for work at night invariably had their rest broken by air raids. Four flights, each of five German aeroplanes, each of which dropped four bombs, came over every night.

Returning to the line at the end of September, the Division took a small part in the battle of Broodseinde. Being on the left of the front attacked, they were only called upon to round off the new battle line. The Battalion as usual assisted in consolidating the ground won.

" POELCAPELLE."

The last action in which the 29th Division took part during the Third Battle of Ypres was fought on the 9th October when, attacking astride the Staden Railway, it gained all its objectives. The following incident, related by Lieutenant Hughes who was wounded on that day, illustrates the way in which a small happening could be magnified out of all proportion to its importance during those exciting imagination-stirring moments of waiting to go into battle. " Zero on the 9th was at 5.20 a.m., and before that hour we were waiting in a trench on the slopes looking down into Langemarck, when a German 'plane suddenly swooped from low clouds to within fifty feet and began spraying

"POELCAPELLE"

us with machine-gun bullets. It was remarkable that only two or three men were hit, but we opened rifle fire at him and he soon disappeared into the early morning mist. It was most disturbing for a few moments, and I recalled having the same feeling of utter helplessness at Montauban in 1916, when an enemy 'plane appeared over our camp dropping flechettes (pointed steel darts). A tin hat seemed very inadequate protection on such occasions!"

As in the previous actions, the 2nd Mons. were actively employed in consolidating the ground won, and in making the roads and tracks passable early for vehicles.

It had thus been present in all three actions of Third Ypres for which battle honours were awarded to the Monmouthshire Regiment. Of these honours, " Ypres, 1917," and " Langemarck, 1917," are borne on the Colours.

"CAMBRAI, 1917."

The Division was relieved in the Poelcapelle sector on 11th October, and after a few days for recuperation at Proven proceeded to a rest area near Arras for training in preparation for their next battle. The 2nd Mons., however, remained in the Ypres district until November 5th, on which date they commenced a march of seven days through Barlin, Arras, and Bapaume to Equancourt, nearly 100 miles. At one place where they halted for the night billeting accommodation was particularly scanty, and the officers were all put up in the local Y.M.C.A. hut. It being the first occasion on which the whole mess had been together since July, 1915, such an opportunity for revelry and laughter was too good to miss, and the night lives as one of the happiest memories of those who were present.

The attack on Cambrai, while it failed in its furthest objectives, was one of the greatest surprises inflicted on the Germans in the war. Masses of tanks and troops had been assembled behind our lines and at a given moment launched off, supported by brigades of artillery hitherto silent and unsuspected. All this needed much preparatory organization, and the failure of the enemy to notice what was going on was due to the loyal obedience of all troops to the instructions issued enjoining secrecy and concealment. Movement and work by day were carefully regulated to what the Germans would normally expect to see: the 2nd Mons., for instance, marched by night from Ypres, hiding up in woods and villages by day; horse lines, always difficult to conceal, were covered with camouflage netting, and, like the great majority of the moving columns, the Battalion thought it was on the way to Italy where the German-Austro army was exploiting its recent success.

On arrival in the Cambrai area, the 2nd Mons. were employed in laying a light railway track right up to the front line, in order that after the attack gun ammunition could be run up in large quantities as far forward as possible. This was all done under cover of darkness, and traces of the work were carefully hidden before daylight.

At dawn on November 20th, the IIIrd and Vth Corps of the British Third Army attacked and, on the IIIrd Corps reaching its objectives about noon, the 29th Division passed through to exploit the breach, gaining by nightfall after considerable fighting Masnieres, Marcoing and Nine Wood, about six miles in advance of the original line. For once the weather was fine and the sun shone on a British attack.

The instructions for the 2nd Mons. for November 20th were typical of the duties allotted to a pioneer unit in the attack. From zero hour onwards, " B ," " C " and " D " Companies were employed in continuing the light railway forward from St. Quentin Mill to La Vaquerie, while "A" Company, under the Divisional Artillery Commander, made tracks for the use of guns forward from the Hindenburg Line. These tasks involved clearing many thick belts of wire, levelling the trench systems where necessary, and filling in shell-holes. In addition, parties were supplied to lay tapes across country to the advanced headquarters of all three infantry brigades, in order to ease the task of runners in finding them by day and night.

One such party, led by Lieutenant W. T. Charles, trailed the G.O.C. of the 88th Brigade. Among its impedimenta was a large notice board, with the legend " 88th Brigade H.Q." in bold lettering. Its conscientious bearer carried it

"CAMBRAI, 1917"

with the lettered side towards the enemy, until the Brigade Major observed it with scandalized horror and addressed him with unmitigated criticism.

Lieutenant Charles relates that during a pause in the advance for the infantry to reform their ranks, he saw a large party of Germans being collected to be led back. Suddenly a hare darted across, and apparently every British soldier in sight went after it, to the stupefaction of the captives. On the hare getting away, however, war was speedily resumed.

Many parts of the ground over which the battle was fought permitted a wide view, and it was a most interesting experience to all ranks to see fighting in the open for the first time, and to judge for themselves the offensive powers of tanks: one officer followed the trail of a tank into a ravine, where he estimated it must have shot up a whole German company, from the number of bodies left there.

Up to November 30th, the Battalion less "A" Company was employed on railway construction. To increase the rate of track laying, the Division ordered that companies so engaged should carry no rifles or equipment other than gas helmets, thus permitting heavier loads of material to be conveyed. All ranks would have preferred carrying their weapons, but in the circumstances they had no option, and in any case it seemed most unlikely that pioneers would require them without some notice.

"A" Company meanwhile was employed on the defences of Masnieres and Marcoing, being accommodated in German dug-outs in their late Hindenburg Line. These dug-outs were particularly elaborate. They were reached by staircases of from 20 to 25 steps down, and consisted of long corridors below ground with rooms leading off. Some were heated by carbon stoves provided with chimneys to clear the fumes, and were lighted, in German times, by electricity. The walls of officers' quarters were lined with panelling evidently taken from churches. Above ground the working parties were much harrassed by trench mortars and machine guns, especially after the first few days when the Germans had taken stock of the new situation.

On November 30th, the enemy counter-attacked in strength all along the front of the salient formed where the British advance had stopped. They succeeded in breaking through on a ten mile stretch immediately on the right of the 29th Division, which held fast to all its positions. The flank was temporarily turned and even Divisional Headquarters at Gouzeaucourt was overrun, the G.O.C. and his staff narrowly escaping capture. Owing to the salient these Headquarters while at normal distance behind their own troops were very close to the rear of the neighbouring division.

"B," "C" and "D" Companies were quartered near Gouzeaucourt but had gone off to their tasks early. About 8 a.m. the handful of details left behind were startled by machine-gun bullets. Almost immediately a soldier of another division ran in, calling out, "The Boche are coming," and sure enough a grey-clad horde of men was seen sweeping over a ridge but a few hundred yards away. Lieutenant Rosenbaum collected as many men as he could, and directed them to Fins where Battalion Headquarters was. Captain C. Comely and several men were wounded and captured, this being the first occasion in which the 2nd Mons. lost prisoners of war.

"B" Company, as has been stated, were proceeding to their work well up in the Cambrai salient, unarmed and with heavy loads of railway material. A thick fog lay on the ground, and the first intimation they had that anything had gone wrong was when half a dozen men came running through it. They were stopped and enquiry revealed the startling news that the Germans had broken through on the right of the 29th Division, and were already in possession of Gouzeaucourt. The company continued towards its task, trusting to arm itself from such dead and wounded as might be found on the field. For a time it came under shell-fire, and when this stopped, the fog lifted at the same time, disclosing strong parties of Germans advancing towards them 400 yards away. The company dumped its material on the spot, and, being unable to do anything else, retired in extended order, keeping their distance of 400 yards from the enemy. Much to their relief they came across Irish Guards marching up in fours who then opened into extended formations and advanced on the enemy as if at Chelsea Barracks. "B" Company volunteered to go with them, chancing to casualties for weapons, but the offer was declined, and the company took advantage of a nearby hill to watch the Guards in action.

This counter-attack, of which the company saw but the fringe, for the whole Guards Division took part, restored the flank of the 29th Division. They retook Gouzeaucourt amongst other places, and recaptured those of the 2nd Mons. who, having been wounded, the Germans had not been able in the short time available to evacuate. Captain C. Comely, who had been severely wounded in the leg, and Captain North were among those thus rescued; their wounds had been dressed by the Germans, who had treated them with every consideration.

" B," " C " and " D " Companies all rejoined headquarters at Fins in the afternoon, and were issued with fresh arms, ammunition and food. Several men of the Battalion who had managed to secure rifles had gone over with the Guards in their attack.

Tremendously heavy fighting for the possession of Masnieres and Marcoing occurred from November 30th to December 3rd, and only the grim determination and dogged tenacity of which the 29th Division was capable held this corner of the salient and averted a crushing defeat from the Third Army. In this the 2nd Mons. had their share, unfortunately not as a battalion but piecemeal as companies were thrown in to assist the worn infantry. "A" Company thus reinforced the K.O.S.B.'s, " B " the Royal Inniskillings, and " C " the S.W.B., only withdrawing with them when the Division retired under orders to the Hindenburg Line. This has made it the more difficult to chronicle the part played by the Battalion, but what happened to "A" Company is probably typical of events in other companies.

Two platoons of "A" Company (Captain F. L. Spencer) had been digging trenches in front of Marcoing, while the other two under Lieutenants Hopkins and Cockrill were on similar work near Masnieres. Lieutenant Hopkins' half-company had been working all night and had just returned to their dug-outs when the alarming news that the whole front was retiring roused them. Lieutenant Cockrill relates that he was a few minutes slower than Hopkins in turning out because he had less clothing on when the alarm was given. On getting up into the trench he found that troops were indeed retiring and

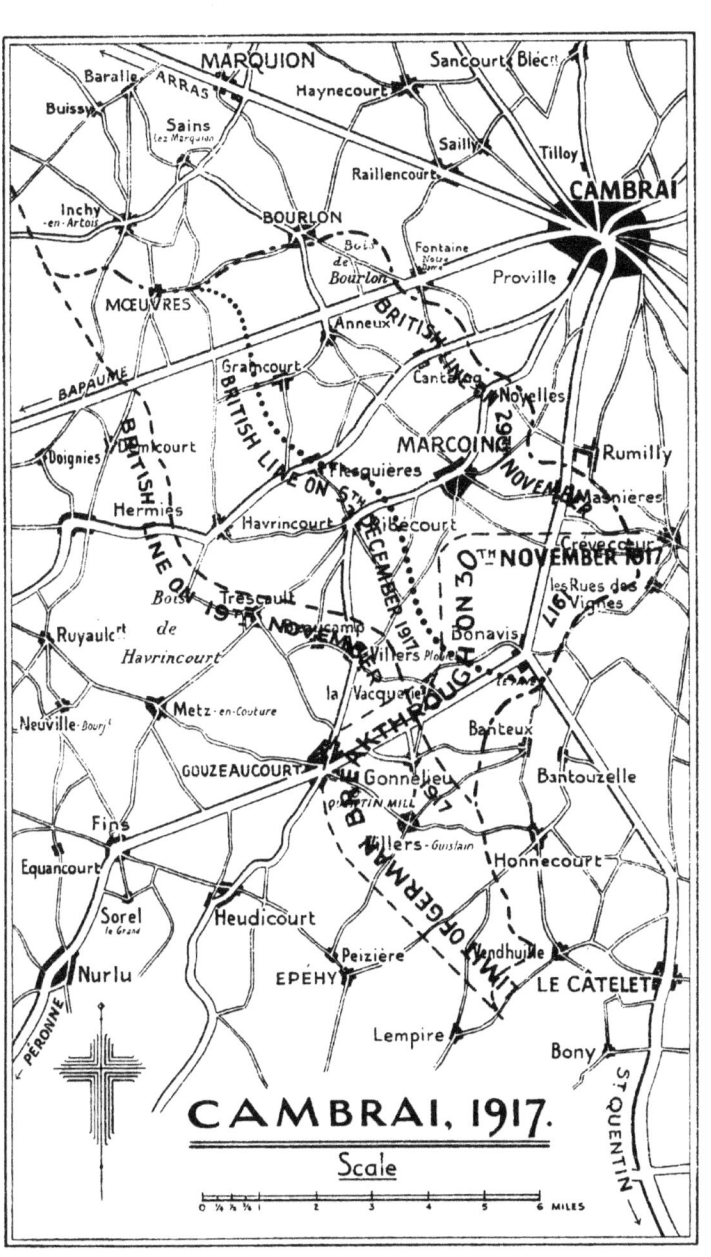

that he was in the midst of machine-gun fire coming from the flank and rear. Searching for his own men, he ran into a party of Germans, exchanged shots with them and " ran like blazes " to where he thought he might find Spencer's half-company. Instead he got into a sunken road where he found Hopkins and a few men, together with a Brigadier, Staff Captain and a machine-gun crew of the 20th Division (the division on the right of the 29th). This mixed party advanced some distance and then got into the very trench which they had been digging during the night.

They manned this trench and another running nearly at right angles to the original line, and were fortunate in finding in front a stretch of formidable German barbed wire. In this wire was a gap which became a veritable deathtrap to the enemy, for Sergeant Cross, the Battalion's crack shot, stood opposite it and shot down man after man as they tried to trickle through.

Several attacks were repulsed that day—as Cockrill puts it, " We were attacked several distinct times that first day and we repulsed each effort, I suppose—anyway these bursts seemed more to fade away than be repulsed. We had a strong position, and had a feeling of security after we got settled down." After dark, German bombers attempted to force their way along the trench, but were checked at a barrier with grenades which somehow the men had managed to find. This was his last effort that night, and in the ensuing comparative quiet the party had time at last to think of the demands made by the inner man. They had had no food since the previous day and the only water to drink had been obtained from a shell-hole. During the night, however, they rejoined under orders Captain Spencer's half-company which, acting with the K.O.S.B.'s, was manning an uncompleted trench near Marcoing.

Daylight found them in inadequate cover with the Germans barely a hundred yards distant. The hostile machine-gunners, as they tried to get into positions from which to bring enfilade fire to bear, afforded excellent targets to such marksmen as Sergeant Cross, and many of them were brought down. Lieutenant Hopkins was wounded by a grenade thrown by an enterprising German who crawled within range, but a worse blow befell the Battalion a few hours later when Captain (Monty)

"CAMBRAI, 1917"

Spencer, a keen, popular and stout-hearted officer, was shot through the head.

Battalion Headquarters accompanied " B " Company in support of the Inniskillings. The orders to move had arrived so late that to gain time the troops marched by compass bearings across country; even so, daylight came with the men marching in fours along the Cambrai road, and with no time to spare to get into any other formation. Happily, no attention was paid to them by the enemy. The Inniskillings C.O. required the company to reinforce his own companies on the further side of a swamp, but routes to the posts were so close to the enemy that no attempt could be made to reach them in daylight, and eventually the company occupied a position in rear which gave facilities for supporting the Irishmen by fire.

On December 4th, the Companies withdrew with the battalions to which they had been attached through a new line which had been built up in rear, and concentrated in Fins, where they unluckily suffered a number of casualties from high velocity shells. " B " Company's mess was struck, and a shell exploded in a cattle shed immediately next to the barn used as Battalion Headquarters. Four cooks of another regiment were killed, but nobody in the Orderly Room hurt, although all, including Colonel Evans, were considerably shaken.

After fourteen days continuous fighting, the rest which was now given to the Division came none too soon. It billetted in the Cauroy area until the 16th and then marched north to Wizerne (the Battalion's first billets of 1914) for the training and absorbtion of drafts.

Sergeants Cross and Wagstaff and Private J. Griffiths were subsequently awarded Military Medals for their conduct in the fighting. The honour " Cambrai, 1917 " on the Colours, earned by the 2nd Battalion, is a mark of high distinction, for no troops gained greater renown at Cambrai than those of the 29th Division.

CHAPTER VII.

YPRES SALIENT
THE BATTLE OF THE LYS.

THE Honours List for New Year, 1918, included M.C.'s for Captains C. Comely and M. F. Turner, D.C.M.'s for C.S.M. Yearsley and Transport Sergeant Roberts, and the M.M. for Sergeant A. E. Smith.

On January 6th the Battalion entrained for Ypres, whence it marched to familiar ground at La Brique. Here it remained for three months working on rearward tasks when its division rested and up forward when it was in the line, which at this period was the Passchaendaele sector.

It was on the whole an uneventful spell. British losses in the battles of 1917 had not been replaced, yet the B.E.F. had been impelled to take over a long frontage from the French. On the other side of No Man's Land, Germany released from the Russian threat was preparing what turned out to be her last throw, and was unwilling to dissipate any strength in minor operations before she was ready for the big attack. The initiative had passed—Germany was gathering up her loins to strike, while the Allies with attenuated numbers waited for the blow.

On 28th February, conforming with the reduction of infantry brigades from four to three battalions, a measure necessitated by the failure of reinforcing drafts to keep pace with casualties, the Battalion was reduced to an establishment of three companies. "D" Company disappeared, its personnel being distributed among the surviving companies.

Headquarters at this time were in a cottage at La Brique built by the Battalion's Pioneer Section from salvaged material, and in later days members of the battalion were interested to note that this edifice survived intact the vicissitudes of the campaign of 1918.

The principal tasks on which the 2nd Monmouths were engaged were the construction of the Goudberg defences, digging and draining the Army Line of Defence near Weiltje, laying and maintaining duckboard tracks in the Divisional area, and making and repairing forward roads.

These tasks included the digging of a series of trenches along the ridge, ironically named Belle Vue, some 150 yards behind the front line. They were intended to serve as battle positions should the forward outposts be driven in, and they could be rapidly manned from German " pill-boxes," now in our hands, which were occupied by the troops in support. Fierce fighting had taken place on the ridge, for every few yards bodies of British or German soldiers were encountered and had to be removed for re-burial.

A road from Gravenstafel to Belle Vue Ridge was also constructed by the Battalion. The terrain was completely pitted with shell-holes and not a square yard of unscarred earth was visible. The first task was to join up a line of shell-holes on each side of the road-site to form a ditch leading the water to the becks; next, holes in the road were drained into the ditch; finally the holes were cleared and filled in. In one hole, full like the others of liquid mud, were found a dead horse and a field gun, which gives an impression of the size of the cavities and the immensity of the task. Objects such as these were removed and the holes filled with fascines and such road material as was available. Transport wagons brought the material as far forward as possible, after which it was man-handled. The task involved marching four or five miles every night, the men laden with rifles, ammunition, picks, shovels and other heavy impedimenta, and working right through the night under shell-fire, for the enemy was not disposed to permit such duties to proceed unhampered.

It is interesting to note that the 2nd Mons. provided the light heavy weight champion of the Second Army in the Army Championship fought in February, 1918.

THE BATTLE OF THE LYS.

On the 21st March the Germans commenced their final bid for victory with a tremendous onslaught on the British

THE BATTLE OF THE LYS

Fifth Army in the Somme area, following it up with a fierce attack in the Lys district on April 9th. The sector attacked on the latter date was occupied by British divisions which, having been badly mauled in the Somme fighting, had been brought up to lick their wounds in a quiet part, and there was also a Portuguese division which had been in the area for some time. The Portuguese gave way to the attack, and a mass of enemy poured through the gap, widening it by turning the flanks of the British defences. So rapid was their progress in the case of the 34th Division, holding the Armentieres sector with originally another division between it and the Portuguese, that its reserves were fighting on its rearward right flank by 10 a.m., while its forward troops had not by that hour been engaged.

The 29th Division at the time was under orders for the Somme, and was in the midst of relief from its quiet portion of the Ypres salient. Under pressure of events in the Second Army area, these orders were countermanded and the Division was hurried piece-meal into the fighting as fast as its formations could move. Two of its brigades fought at Estaires, and the 88th Brigade with the Pioneer Battalion were sent to the assistance of the hard-pressed but stubborn 34th Division. The Battalion had gone to School Camp near Poperinghe on the 8th April in anticipation of the relief of the Division. On the 10th it was directed to proceed with the 88th Brigade (Brigadier-General B. Freyburg, V.C.), which passed under control of the 34th Division, at this time engaged in fighting a rear-guard action with the enemy pressing on both flanks.

The 2nd Mons. embussed about mid-day and many were the jokes on getting a ride at last instead of having to walk, while some optimists endeavoured to collect fares. As the column of busses proceeded from Bailleul towards Armentieres French peasants were met streaming down the road, pushing hand-carts and prams, and leading dogs drawing little carts, all laden with packages; these were refugees fleeing from their homes on hearing the Germans were close at hand, taking with them such belongings as they could. The busses, making slow progress through the press of peasants and transport, continued along the road until at about 5 p.m. near La Creche they were fired upon by German scouts. The Battalion promptly debussed and was ordered to entrench in the immediate vicinity. While officers were laying tapes to mark the line, it was found necessary to despatch a small party to clear enemy snipers out of a spinney, from which they were making themselves troublesome, but before the traces had been completed a staff officer arrived with orders for the Battalion to construct and occupy posts south of the road about Papot, Pont d'Achelles and De Seule facing Steenwercke.

Under these instructions " B " Company (Captain Foster) went to the cross-roads at Pont d'Achelles. Although it was still daylight, wounded men passing through on their way to the rear were unable to indicate the direction from which German attack might be expected, but as the heaviest fire sounded on the right of the road " B " Company moved along it in that direction towards Papot, until they found a suitable field of fire, where they dug in. Two men went into the hamlets of Pont d'Achelles and Rabot, and smashed every bottle of intoxicants they could find. In Rabot a party of four Germans was met; both parties were extremely surprised, but the Germans recovered first and took to their heels. This incident showed that if there were a line in front, it had gaps in it.

By dusk on the 10th the enemy advance, having worked round to the right rear of the 34th Division, was threatening to cut the Bailleul-Armentieres road, but a determined counter-attack by a hastily collected mixed force stemmed them for a time. The 2nd Monmouthshires then relieved two companies of Royal Engineers, who were clinging tenaciously to a line of posts about Rabot, it being recorded by the historian of the 34th Division that " thus for the third time was the Boche held up when a break through seemed imminent." With the enemy thus active on his right and the division on his left losing ground, the G.O.C. 34th Division managed to complete during the night his withdrawal to the north bank of the Lys. So far as the Battalion was concerned, the night proved to be fairly quiet and by morning the three companies had connected up their lines and were holding a strong position.

As dawn came, very heavy fire commenced in the valley in front of " B " Company's position; a little later it was suddenly realized that bullets were also being fired into their backs from

Pont d'Achelles in rear. Two sets of messages were sent to Headquarters with this information, and the company with bayonets fixed climbed out of its trench and moved through the houses of Pont d'Achelles. No enemy was encountered there, but as the men went through the furthest buildings, a company of Hampshires met them coming from Bailleul direction. Apparently the brigade responsible for the area had observed the German movements, and had sent this company to resist their advance. The Hampshires would not give way to " B " Company, nor " B " to them : both commanders blew their whistles therefore, and the two companies moved on completely intermixed and cleared up the ground to the next village, Papot. On arrival here a runner came from Headquarters with orders to dig in facing the village, while the Hampshires were instructed to rejoin their battalion which was understood to be beyond the village, and they accordingly departed. "A" and " C " Companies came up almost immediately and the men started to dig in, but Germans returned to the village after the Hampshires had passed and opened machine-gun fire, as the men lay scratching shelter for themselves with their entrenching tools. The stay here, however, was not long.

Forward troops of the 34th Division had been holding during the night a pronounced salient jutting forward a mile or so south-east of Pont d'Achelles. It was foreseen that this position was untenable for any length of time, and about noon the 2nd Mons. were ordered to construct a line of defence between Papot and Rue de Sac, through which the forward troops were to retire after dusk. So confused was the situation that the Battalion was ordered to attack if necessary to gain this line as it was considered of vital importance. The area was, however, occupied without difficulty by 3.30 p.m., "A" Company being on the right, " B " on the left and " C " in support, and wagons arrived in good time with picks and shovels; but they had hardly commenced to entrench when the forward troops started coming back. As they passed through the right of the Battalion, they spread the rumour that a general withdrawal had been ordered, and a portion of "A" Company not unnaturally went with them. Fortunately Battalion Headquarters was on the alert, and on their explaining to the men

THE BATTLE OF THE LYS

that the retirement orders did not apply to the 2nd Monmouthshires, they returned at once and resumed their tasks. The Boche followed close behind the retiring troops, but made no attempt to press beyond the Monmouthshire trenches. They shelled, however, and one unlucky hit alone killed and wounded 16 men of one platoon of " B " Company. When these trenches had been almost completed, it was found that there were no troops on the left flank. After a conference at Headquarters, "A" and " C " Companies were directed to remain in their present trenches, while " B " Company fell back at an angle of 45 degrees to form a defensive flank. The men were too tired to dig any more, having since the previous day made two sets of trenches and moved several times with no rests in between, and they therefore occupied a ditch running along the general line, scratching some of the earth out to improve the position slightly.

During the night orders were received that the ground was to be held at all costs. Worried about his left flank, where troops of the 25th Division were supposed to be, Colonel Evans visited at midnight the commanding officer of the neighbouring battalion, and found that his posts were considerably distant from and to the rear of " B " Company's left. He was unable to induce the officer concerned to move his men to gain touch with " B " Company, and was compelled to send two platoons of " C " Company to fill a portion of the gap.

Later, orders came for the Battalion to extend its right south of the main road to gain contact with the 2nd Hampshires. Another platoon of " C " Company was detailed for this purpose and ordered to construct a post. But similar conditions ruled on this flank: the Hampshires were found to be back at a mill several hundred yards in right rear of the Battalion and connection was therefore impossible. There were two places named Papot and one Rabot within a mile and a half and possibly confusion had arisen in the orders to battalions, but at all events, without reckoning the extensions right and left, the 2nd Monmouthshires had already been allotted a frontage of over a thousand yards, with only three instead of the usual four companies to hold it. After a trying night, therefore, they faced dawn of the 12th April holding a salient position with a thin line, their right flank open and their left weak, and with only one platoon in reserve.

The enemy attacked early on the 12th all along the Brigade front, which extended from Steenwercke Station on the right to the 2nd Mons. positions from Pont d'Achelles to Rue de Sac. From his headquarters Colonel Evans could see German troops passing in streams under a bridge in the vicinity of Rabot, and from " B " Company's area even their guns could be seen in action. The weight of the attacks, which persisted all through the morning, fell on Pont d'Achelles, but " this part of the line," says the historian of the 34th Division, " was held by the Monmouths who maintained their position well, in spite of early in the attack losing four officers and seventy-five other ranks from trench-mortar and machine-gun fire." At first the stretcher bearers were able to evacuate the wounded, but the bombardment grew to such intensity that after a time it was impossible to travel ten yards over the top without being shot down, and the wounded therefore had to remain where they fell. Eventually the Boche came over in large numbers, but rapid fire by rifles and Lewis guns stopped them. They then abandoned attacking in waves, and their men instead trickled forward in twos and threes from cover to cover, looking for gaps in the line.

About mid-day the Brigade Major informed Colonel Evans that instructions had been received for the line to be held for a further twenty-four hours, that a company of the Royal Newfoundland Regiment was coming up in support at once, and that the remainder of that battalion would arrive later. The two C.O.'s were to form a combined headquarters at a dugout in a light railway embankment about half a mile in rear, and he asked what time Colonel Evans would go back so that he could arrange with Colonel Woodruffe of the Newfoundlands. In view of later events the hour selected by Colonel Evans, 4 p.m., was to prove a singularly lucky choice.

Throughout the morning and early afternoon the Battalion, although continually plastered by trench-mortars and harassed by machine-guns, warded off the enemy's infantry. Many casualties had been received, but all ranks felt that they were giving the enemy " as good as they got." About twenty minutes to 4 p.m. the Adjutant, Captain Ibbs, reminded Colonel Evans

THE BATTLE OF THE LYS

of his appointment, and battalion headquarters moved off to the rendezvous. The two commanding officers conferred for about a quarter of an hour, and then satisfied with their arrangements, came up from the dugout. To their amazement they found a mixed lot of Monmouths and Newfoundlands retiring upon them, pursued by the enemy. The men were easily rallied behind the embankment and the German advance was stayed.

What had happened was the consequence of the two weak flanks. Early in the afternoon the enemy extended his operations by attacking the weak 25th Division on the left and made considerable progress. Nothing had been done to stop his infiltration on the right, and at 4 p.m. the Germans closed the pincers on the Battalion. An attack in great strength was launched against Pont d'Achelles and near Lampernisse, right and left of the position; the enemy broke through round both flanks, and eight officers and some four hundred men who refused to give ground were cut off, a fate which headquarters would almost certainly have shared but for their move.

"B" Company's Lewis guns had run out of ammunition about mid-day and the magazines could not be replenished because carrying parties were all shot down. Rifle ammunition, too, had to be carefully husbanded, and the men were warned to reserve their fire for good targets. When the final attack came, they saw "A" and "C" Companies move after a time to the rear, but they held their own ground, and watched the enemy sweeping round both flanks out of effective rifle range.

Some little time later Captain Foster counted the numbers still in the ditch and, finding the ammunition very low, gave orders to retire, but their retreat had been cut off, and with a great number of men of the other companies they were rounded up. Captain Foster, writing to Colonel Evans soon after his capture, said :—" I tried or rather wanted to reinforce the people on my right, but before I could do so I saw the troops on my left retiring. Our front we had kept clear, but our lines were enfiladed from both flanks, and we, being almost sideways to the main attack, could not bring sufficient fire to bear. Enemy machine guns were already in the road behind us. However I am quite satisfied with the damage we did—the men proved themselves splendid and disciplined soldiers "

THE BATTLE OF THE LYS

The remnants of the Battalion held the embankment in conjunction with the Newfoundlanders until midnight when they were ordered to dig themselves in about La Creche in support to the Brigade, Colonel Evans' bayonet strength having now been reduced to about one hundred and fifty, with four officers.

The Battalion Lewis Gun Officer, Lieutenant I. E. Owen, was among those who fell in this fighting. He had been in France a considerable time and was regarded with special affection by all ranks, for during periods of rest " Dicky " Owen had been indefatigable in arranging boxing contests and other amusements. He was mortally wounded while rallying the men during the enemy break-through of the 12th April.

Colonel Evans relates that the most heroic act he saw in the war occurred while he was at the railway embankment. During the retirement one of his officers fell shot in the head about fifty yards in front. He was seen to move several times, but owing to the inferno of fire attempt at rescue seemed doomed to failure. Beside Colonel Evans stood a Newfoundland sergeant, whose name he never knew. Watching the spasmodic movements of the wounded officer, he said at length, " I can't stick it any longer, sir ; I'm going," and despite the remonstrance of the colonel, who felt it to be the inevitable sacrifice of a gallant life, over he went. Crawling, wriggling from shell-hole to shell-hole, he reached the officer, and in the same laborious way brought him back, although he saw the wounds must be fatal.

The Battalion remained at La Creche until about 9 p.m. on the 13th when it moved forward under orders to cover the withdrawal of the Brigade. About midnight, the completion of the retirement having been reported, the Battalion moved off, but finding shortly afterwards that the troops had not entirely withdrawn, the companies were halted and ordered to occupy trenches in the immediate vicinity. At 2 a.m., word having come that the troops were clear, the Battalion resumed its march, reaching the position allotted to it on the Ravelsberg Ridge, east of Bailleul, about two hours later. The whole retirement was unmolested by organized parties of the enemy, but three Germans, over impetuous in scouting, ran into the Battalion and were taken prisoner.

THE BATTLE OF THE LYS

Severe fighting, in which but for artillery fire, the 88th Brigade was scarcely involved, occurred again on the 14th, but the 34th Division, its flanks having now been secured by fresh troops, maintained its positions intact, and during the night, with its attached brigades of which there were no fewer than three, it was relieved by the 59th Division, the 2nd Monmouthshires going back to Croix de Poperinghe. The extent of the casualties may be measured by the fact that one battalion of the 59th Division sufficed to relieve the 88th Brigade.

Two hours after the relief, however, the enemy attacking in force with fresh troops broke through the 59th Division, completely wiping out the battalion which had relieved the 88th Brigade, and the 34th Division found itself again standing up to his assaults, although now with Bailleul in front instead of behind them. The 2nd Mons. were moved to a position behind the Division's left with orders to co-operate with the 4th Worcesters should the course of events compel that unit to counter-attack. The enemy had, however, exhausted himself with the capture of Bailleul, and serious fighting gradually died down, both sides contenting themselves with struggles for local tactical features rather than operations on a grand scale. The 88th Brigade remained in the line incessantly scrapping, its battalions relieving each other in rotation, until French troops took over the Divisional front on the 20th April, when the Battalion marched back to a camp near Staples. During this latter period in the line, the 2nd Mons., being in support to the Brigade, supplied working parties to each of the battalions in the trenches.

Thus came to an end the most severe fighting which the 2nd Monmouthshires experienced in the whole of the war. Employed on pioneer duties for the two previous years, with little experience of the ordinary role of infantry and none of a war of movement, it had been called upon without warning to stand up to first class fighting troops, fully trained in open warfare. Fighting on the defensive calls for higher degrees of courage and endurance than fighting in the offensive, and the Battalion emerged from its ordeal battered in body but unbeaten in spirit. For the second time the Pioneers had been called upon, as the Divisional reserve, to help to check the enemy.

THE BATTLE OF THE LYS

Comedy often obtrudes in the midst of tragedy, and, fortunately for the sanity of those who fought in France, the dark side was sometimes lit by flashes, absurd or comical, most of them too trivial to record, which served then to distract the mind, if but for a moment, from the seeming hopelessness of things, and which even now bring chuckles of recollection from those who participated in them. While the retirement from La Creche was taking place, there occurred one such incident, which, while regarded unhappily by the individuals concerned, lost nothing in amusement as the story spread around.

When the move was ordered, Colonel Evans' servant, laudably desirous of leaving no spoils to the enemy, helped himself too liberally to the contents of a rum jar, with the result that an escort had to be told off to look after him. The route led through some marshy ground, and the unlucky man, having already metaphorically strayed from the strait and narrow path, now did so literally into thigh-deep mud, from which all the efforts of his escort, worried sufficiently by the increasing proximity of the pursuit, could not extricate him in the few minutes at their disposal. He had to be abandoned to the Germans, who having more time and less worry eventually got him out. The other unfortunate was the Colonel, for his field glasses, shaving kit, spare socks and shirt all went to Germany in his servant's haversack.

AFTER THE BATTLE

On 21st April the Battalion embussed and rejoined the 29th Division at Hondeghem. For a few days it rested, bathing and re-equipping the men, and doing little more than reorganize. Then on the 26th it commenced work on construction and wiring the 2nd Zone of Defence. On the following day the Division re-entered the line, taking over the sector from Nieppe Forest to the Hazebrouck-Bailleul railway, and the 2nd Mons. moved up to the L'Hoffand area, near Hazebrouck, where they remained until June 20th, working principally on the rearward defences, and being constantly harassed by gas-shell bombardments which took their toll of casualties. The fact that the

British line had been pushed back a considerable distance meant, however, that the men were now in better country, away from areas where shells had left nothing but death and destruction, and these pleasanter conditions were very helpful in restoring their health and spirits.

This Divisional tour was not altogether quiescent, for on the 4th June " C " Company was employed on the consolidation of ground captured on the previous day by Royal and Dublin Fusiliers. Work was interrupted by heavy barrage fire and hampered by lack of infantry carrying parties, but continued until nearly dawn. Major A. H. Edwards, M.C., who had been with the Battalion almost continuously since 1914, was severely wounded in the course of this operation. Captain T. L. Ibbs, M.C., who had been Adjutant since 1915, was promoted Major, Captain R. T. Saunders becoming Adjutant in his place.

D.C.M.'s were awarded in June to two Sergeants of the same name, W. Williams, their numbers being 265503 and 265363. The latter, who already had the M.M., was a truly remarkable character, of whom it is not necessary to recount any special deed of gallantry, for he was always willing to tackle nasty jobs. His general attitude towards war was different from the average man's : he appeared to take a real interest in it and positively to enjoy patrolling in No Man's Land or leading a bombing party. More than that, he appeared to infuse his outlook into others, for—there was no need to ask for volunteers —men went with him on such enterprises because they liked them ! Sergeant Williams carried out these tasks without recklessness but with all the craft and foresight of the hunter or poacher, as many a luckless German found to his cost. He had joined the Battalion before the war, after service with regular gunners, and served with it throughout, his long, spare figure, surmounted by its sandy top, being regarded with special affection by all ranks. He received another decoration, the French Croix de Guerre, at the end of the year.

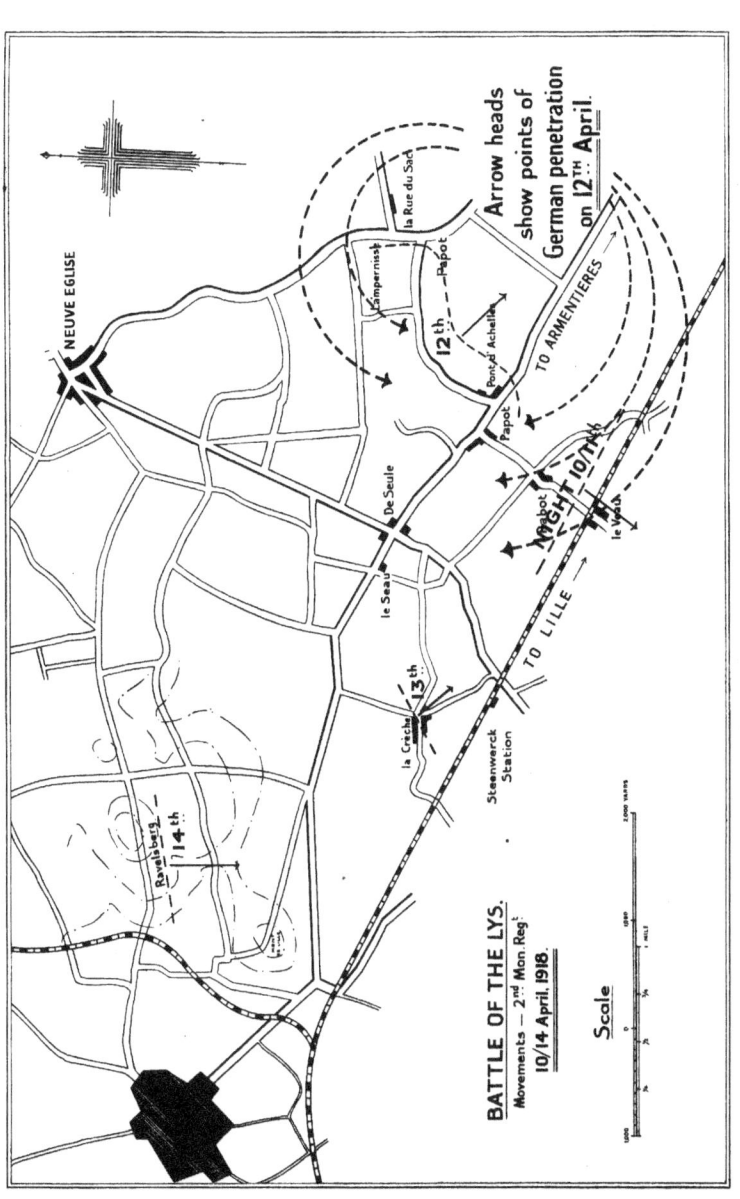

CHAPTER VIII.

THE TURNING OF THE TIDE—OUTTERSTEENE—STEENWERCKE—"YPRES, 1918"—"MESSINES, 1918"—"COURTRAI"—THE ARMISTICE—THE MARCH INTO GERMANY—PONTYPOOL ONCE MORE.

THE TURNING OF THE TIDE.

THE Division was relieved on the 20th June for rest and training, the Battalion going into camp near Staples. A Divisional Horse Show was held on 9th July, at which Lieutenant F. H. Wigmore obtained the second prize for jumping and Transport Sergeant J. Roberts the first prize for "the best turned-out mounted N.C.O. in the Division"; the third prize for other ranks jumping also came to the Battalion. At the Divisional Boxing Contest, held in the same month, the 2nd Mons. won the light weight championship. During this rest period one company at a time was employed on the Hazebrouck defences.

On July 22nd a move was made to Noordepeine, where companies were billeted in somewhat congested conditions among farms. Training was continued until the 25th when the Battalion marched to Eecke, where tents were drawn and camps pitched, each company being in a separate field, for they were now within artillery range.

The 2nd Monmouthshires came temporarily under orders of the Xth Corps Signals, and were employed for several nights in digging a cable trench over the famous Mont des Cats and forward from there to artillery headquarters. On the Division taking over the Merris sector on 2nd August, Battalion Headquarters went with "C" Company to Le Peuplier, while "A" proceeded to Court Croix and "B" to Pradelles where they settled down in rearward defended localities, and resumed their normal role of divisional pioneers. On 10th August the Battalion moved back to the L'Hoffand area, but for a week continued to send parties forward to work on the communication trenches in the Merris sector.

OUTTERSTEENE.

The 87th Brigade (temporarily commanded by Lieutenant-Colonel G. T. Raikes, D.S.O., South Wales Borderers) attacked the Outtersteene Ridge on the 18th August, and two platoons of "A" Company accompanied the K.O.S.B. over the top, their orders being to assist in the consolidation of the captured ground. Capture of the ridge would permit observation over much of the country towards the River Lys, and it was expected to be strongly held and sternly defended. A scheme of artillery barrage had been prepared to cover every square yard of ground, through which, it was confidently stated, no living person could move, a boast which was soon verified. Superimposed upon this was a machine-gun barrage. There was to be no preliminary bombardment but the assaulting troops were to leave their trenches at the exact moment the barrage commenced; the attack was timed for 11 a.m. on the 18th, and the men moved into the jumping-off trenches during the previous night. Lieutenant H. J. Hopkins in command, Lieutenant R. H. Watkins and eighty-five N.C.O.'s and men of "A" Company, 2nd Mons., were to carry barbed wire and spades, keeping close up to Captain Hayton's company of the K.O.S.B.

Lieutenant Hopkins describes the scene before the action as follows : " Company headquarters were at a farm at Stella Crossing on the Merris-Outtersteene road. It commanded an excellent view of the surrounding country, which was exceedingly picturesque. At the time the corn was almost ripe, standing quite four feet high, and although farming had ceased through the evacuation of the peasantry, the countryside had that calm and peaceful appearance of a typical Belgian harvest-tide. Shell-holes and the usual marks of warfare were hidden by the tall, ripening corn which coloured the landscape.

OUTTERSTEENE

"Looking towards Outtersteene, the scene presented a complete contrast. No Man's Land and the area in front and behind showed the picture so common to the eye of the British soldier—smashed houses, shell-torn soil, discarded limbers, graves with wooden crosses and the waving lines of upturned earth of the trenches. To the left front the ground sloped down to Meteren, a heap of tumbled masonry. In the foreground the Meteren Becque rippled over the worn stones, its water sparkling in the sun as it splashed on its course. On the right the ground rose gradually to where Merris once stood, now ruins in the debris of battle."

On the evening of the 17th, while the setting sun bathed the countryside in a glorious red blaze, the party fell in and moved off to Meteren Bridge, where coils of barbed wire were collected from an Engineer dump. Laden with these, they made their way to African Trench, where they rested for the night, pulling camouflage screens over the trench at dawn to hide themselves from hostile aircraft. The hours crawled by until 11 a.m. when the opening crash of the British barrage sounded the advance to the K.O.S.B. and the Monmouths.

The two platoons, going forward with the K.O.S.B., were impressed with the accuracy of the barrage, which swept every yard of soil in front of them. Then the enemy's counter-barrage came, causing many casualties. The troops held their course steadily behind the wall of our shells regardless of losses, and found themselves eventually among machine-gun posts. Here they were checked momentarily, but a bayonet rush cleared the way. Seeing a gap in the K.O.S.B.'s line, which had been considerably thinned, Lieutenant Watkins led his platoon forward at the double and filled it, being rewarded by a shout of "Well done, Mons.," from Captain Hayton.

The barrage having halted at the foot of the Outtersteene Ridge to allow of the infantry keeping pace with it, Hayton came over to Watkins to check his position by the map. In a few minutes, "like a living thing," the wall of shells and torrent of machine-gun bullets wheeled left, the troops following suit as it moved away from them. Halfway up the hill several Germans emerged from dugouts and surrendered—after the barrage they had little fight left in them, and on the north edge of Outtersteene village Watkins and his men rushed a machine-gun post, capturing an officer, several men and two guns, while further on they secured a major and many men of the 49th Saxon Regiment.

"From the ruins of Outtersteene which was being heavily shelled," writes Watkins, "a strange figure ran towards us, a demented nerve-racked German soldier, with a bandage round his forehead. He was right in the middle of the barrage, with shells crashing all round him, as he ran this way and that trying to dodge them, screaming in his agonized terror. A cry went up, " Don't shoot him!" and in spite of the hellish fire he managed to get to me without serious injury. He fell on his knees and, with tears in his eyes, cried "Kamerad, Offizier! Ich Frau und acht Kinder haben." (Comrade, Officer! I have a wife and eight children.) I pointed to the rear and sent him back as a prisoner."

The objective having been gained, Lieutenant Hopkins set about consolidating the position and in less than five hours a trench had been dug to the required depth and every man was well under cover from machine-gun fire. The wiring in front was carried out under Sergeant Dallimore, and a machine gun with ammunition captured from the enemy was mounted by Lieutenant Watkins in readiness for the expected counter-attack. When the work of consolidation was completed, the K.O.S.B. company commander asked if the Monmouths would remain to help him to hold the line, his own numbers having been considerably reduced, and Hopkins at once agreed. Throughout the afternoon the enemy shelled the positions, and about 5 p.m. three German airmen dived and opened machine-gun fire at them. The K.O.S.B.'s again lost some men, but the airmen soon came to grief, for they were attacked by five or six British aeroplanes who sent them all down in flames.

About 6 p.m. the K.O.S.B.'s requested the party to go out in front to watch for any enemy who might come, in order to give the rest of the troops warning. Hopkins again agreed and without loss of time led them over the top. They advanced over the shell-torn soil to a point about 350 yards in front where they found favourable positions for rifle fire. Here, being now only 24 strong, they formed two mutually supporting posts.

OUTTERSTEENE

At 9 p.m. the German gunners opened barrage fire on the posts and commenced their counter-attack. The 2nd Mons. dropped their shovels, picked up their rifles and directed steady fire on the advancing infantry. The shouts of their officers urging the men on could be heard, but they never approached nearer than a hundred yards from the posts because our artillery had their range accurately and played havoc with their massed formations. Darkness came with the 2nd Mons. still in their posts, streams of shells pouring over their heads. Hopkins was struck on the head in this action by shrapnel and owes his life to his steel helmet; fortunately, although dazed for a time, he was able to carry on. About midnight the party was relieved by K.O.S.B.'s and marched back to rejoin the Battalion, having lost altogether 53 of their numbers killed, wounded or gassed.

For their gallantry and leadership in this action, Lieutenant Hopkins was awarded the M.C., and Sergeant Dallimore and Corporal Belli the M.M.

While half of "A" Company was thus engaged, the remainder of the Battalion stood by for consolidation duties. They were held up for a time by heavy shell-fire but started work after dusk and remained out constructing and wiring strong-posts until after dawn. On the 19th, ground to the south of Outtersteene Ridge was attacked, the Battalion being employed throughout the night on consolidation work. The remainder of the month was spent in improving and wiring the trenches, headquarters moving to Pradelles while the companies were still further forward.

The heavy blows dealt to the enemy throughout August by the British on the Somme front began to show plainly their far-reaching effect, for he made no serious attempt to recover the ground seized from him in the Bailleul sector, and on August 30th his troops were found to have evacuated the salient and, opposite the 29th Division, to have retired about five miles. The Pioneers were at once employed on getting the forward roads in a fit state for the heavy traffic which follows an army, and their almost daily moves of headquarters further forward testify to the progress made.

On September 1st, a platoon of "A" Company, under Lieutenant R. H. Watkins, put in a morning of varied adventure typical of the pursuit so far as the Battalion was concerned. They had been detailed to bridge the Stil Beque stream at Steenwercke and started off to their task early. On the way they came in for the usual shelling and, before reaching the village, had to clear several formidable wire entanglements from the road. While engaged on the wire they were troubled by German shrapnel directed at British aeroplanes actively patrolling overhead, and many large lumps of metal thudded into the ground near them. Then one of the 'planes was forced down near the party. After running a few yards, it caught its nose in a belt of wire and turned half over. Its two occupants crawled out and quite nonchalantly strolled across to ask for a guard for the machine. A man was detailed and the airmen gave Watkins information as to the enemy's movements and warned him to beware of mines in Steenwercke.

The wire having been cut through and piled clear of the road, the platoon proceeded to the village, on the further side of which they could see outposts of the South Wales Borderers. On reaching Steenwercke, Lieutenant Hopkins and Sergeant Parsons went ahead to explore, warning the men on no account to enter buildings because of the danger of mines. They traversed their way along the main street, past houses where smouldering fires indicated the recentness of the German departure, and across the square where the imposing calm majesty of Steenwercke's undamaged church offered striking contrast to its surroundings of smashed walls, toppling roofs, shell-holes and debris. At the eastern end of the village they were fired upon from buildings beyond, known under the sinister name of Murder Farm, but satisfied that there were no Germans in Steenwercke they returned to the platoon and led the men to the bridge site.

Nearby stood a brewery, and from its cellars and vat-rooms they obtained steel rails for use as girders. Over these they placed beams and planks as cross-stays, and were getting well forward with the work when the enemy commenced to shell the place. One shell pitched within ten yards of the party, blowing a huge crater but without inflicting casualties or damaging the bridge. The work went on through the morning, interrupted at intervals by the party making hasty dashes to the cover of a convenient wall when the warning " boom " of the German heavies, firing in salvos, gave notice of an impending crash of shells. Two nearby houses blew up under delayed action mines, machine-gun bullets spattered fitfully on the walls, but the bridge made steady progress. Stones were collected and laid for metalling, and about noon with a final binding of loose earth the task was completed. Soon afterwards, on their way back, the platoon had the satisfaction of meeting guns moving forward to make use of their bridge.

On September 5th the Battalion was once more at La Creche, near the scene of its ordeal of April 12th, and the thoughts of survivors of that fight as they passed again over the field, this time with victory on their side, were stirred by memories of those who fell when defeat seemed so near.

The Division was relieved on the 11th, and the Battalion went back to Hazebrouck for training and refitting, moving again on the 16th to the Road Camp at St. Jan Ter Beizen. Troops were now gathering for extensive operations to be undertaken in conjunction with the Belgian Army for the driving back of the enemy from Belgium, the series of actions for which the Battle Honour " Ypres, 1918 " was awarded.

" MESSINES, 1918."

On September 21st the Division moved north, taking over the sector east of Ypres between the Zillebeek Lake and the Menin Road, the 2nd Mons. going to Brandhoek, " B " Company having preceded them a day earlier into Ypres itself. Work for the attack was begun at once, principally on getting the roads ready for artillery and transport.

The attack began on 28th September and by the end of the day the Division had advanced five miles, capturing Gheluvelt. As usual in the great Salient, rain fell with the opening barrage and the ground rapidly became a morass. Opening the roads and tracks and keeping them fit for traffic became more than ever a paramount necessity if unremitting pressure were to be kept on the enemy, and the 2nd Monmouthshires were engaged to the fullest extent on these duties. On October 2nd the outskirts of Gheluwe were reached, and two days later the Division was relieved for a short rest, having covered in five days much more ground than had been taken in five months in the battles of " Ypres, 1917." During this rest the Battalion remained at Ypres, working on the Menin road.

" COURTRAI."

The Division returned to the line in time for the Battle of Courtrai, which commenced on October 14th. Throughout this battle, in which the Division attacked at Ledeghem, the Monmouthshires moved close behind the attacking troops, working on roads and assisting the engineers to build bridges, and later they repaired railway lines where the Germans had exploded mines. In the initial stages of the attack a platoon of each of "A" and " B " Companies went over with the first waves of infantry to lay foot-bridges to assist them over the Heulebeck stream.

" B " Company's platoon under Lieutenant J. T. Phillips set off at about 1 p.m. on the 13th to the appropriate inspiration of selections from the then popular London revue " Going Up," played on the mess gramophone. The guide supplied by the Leinster Regiment, to which the platoon was being attached for duty, lost his way, with the result that it was midnight before the platoon had picked up its foot-bridges—elongated duck-boards, 12 to 14 feet in length—and settled down in a trench which they had to dig for themselves.

The artillery barrage came down a few minutes before zero, 5 a.m., and the platoon with its bridges went off with the leading files of the Leinsters. Ledeghem was passed without encountering any enemy, although the next following wave of troops had to fight their way, the Germans having by that time emerged from the dugouts to which the barrage had driven them.

Beyond Ledeghem open country was reached, and here, after a time, progress was checked temporarily by heavy artillery

"COURTRAI"

and machine-gun fire, and also because of a thick smoke screen put down by the enemy. Nearly half the platoon was lost in killed and wounded during this check, and when the smoke cleared Phillips had several men under him who had got separated from their own units. The Heulebeck, about a mile from the starting line, was at length reached in front of the infantry, and the bridges were promptly thrown across for them.

Several little disorganized parties of Germans had been met, but only one of them, a machine-gun post of a dozen men, showed fight. Sergeant Dowding ran forward and rushed this party on his own, and in all the platoon collected about thirty prisoners when it started back to rejoin the Battalion.

Sergeant Dowding was given an immediate award of the D.C.M., and Sergeant Hayes, who was also in the party, received the same decoration in the next New Year's honours in recognition of his long record of devotion to duty.

At the crossing of the Lys on October 20th the Battalion was employed in laying pontoon bridges in conjunction with the engineers and in constructing approaches to these bridges. The Germans were by now in full retreat and the chief problem before the British staffs was how to keep up with them. The advance was over undamaged country, through villages and towns whose inhabitants, freed at last from enemy domination, could not do enough for their deliverers.

On November 5th, the Battalion being then at St. Andre, the officers dined together to celebrate the anniversary of the departure of the 2nd Monmouthshires for France in 1914, and a concert for the men was arranged.

The Division was ordered to take part in an attack on a large scale two days later, involving the crossing of the River Scheldt, but the enemy, contrary to expectation, withdrew without contesting this obstacle. On 11th November the Battalion was on the march and had reached Celles when a message was received notifying the cessation of hostilities at 11 a.m., an armistice having been granted to the enemy. It was generally known that the German Government had commenced suing for peace on October 13th, and the information that the first steps had been taken was received with jubilation.

"COURTRAI"

The message signifying this momentous event was sent to Battalion Headquarters by the Divisional staff on the usual form (A.F. C 2121), and ran as follows :—"Hostilities will cease at 1100 AAA 88th Bde will establish outposts on line of RIVER DENDRE AAA 87th and 86th will stand fast on present positions AAA Defensive precautions will be maintained AAA There will be no intercourse of any description with enemy AAA CRE will concentrate all energies on communications indenting on this office for any infantry parties required."

THE MARCH TO GERMANY.

As may be gathered from the last sentence of the message, the 2nd Mons. were put on to road repairs without delay, but on the 14th they marched to Marais A L'Eau : the 29th Division had been selected as one of the two divisions which, preceded by the 2nd Cavalry Brigade, were to lead the advance into Germany. The next few days were spent in re-equipping the men, while lectures were given regarding the attitude to be adopted by the troops on entering German territory.

The march of 178 miles to Cologne commenced on November 18th, and it continued by fairly easy stages until December 1st. The route led near Waterloo, where the G.O.C. gave a lecture to all available officers on Wellington's battle. During a day's halt, on 22nd November, four officers of the Battalion were privileged to visit Brussels to witness the return of King Albert to his capital.

For the last few days of the march a company was attached to the advanced guard of each brigade, for the Division was marching on two parallel roads, to clear any obstacles which might be encountered. Everywhere the troops were welcomed by Belgians overjoyed to see those who had at last delivered them from the German yoke, and some of the happiest memories of those who served in the Battalion are connected with this historic march. They had little to give, these unfortunate people, but all that they had they placed at the disposal of the conquering troops.

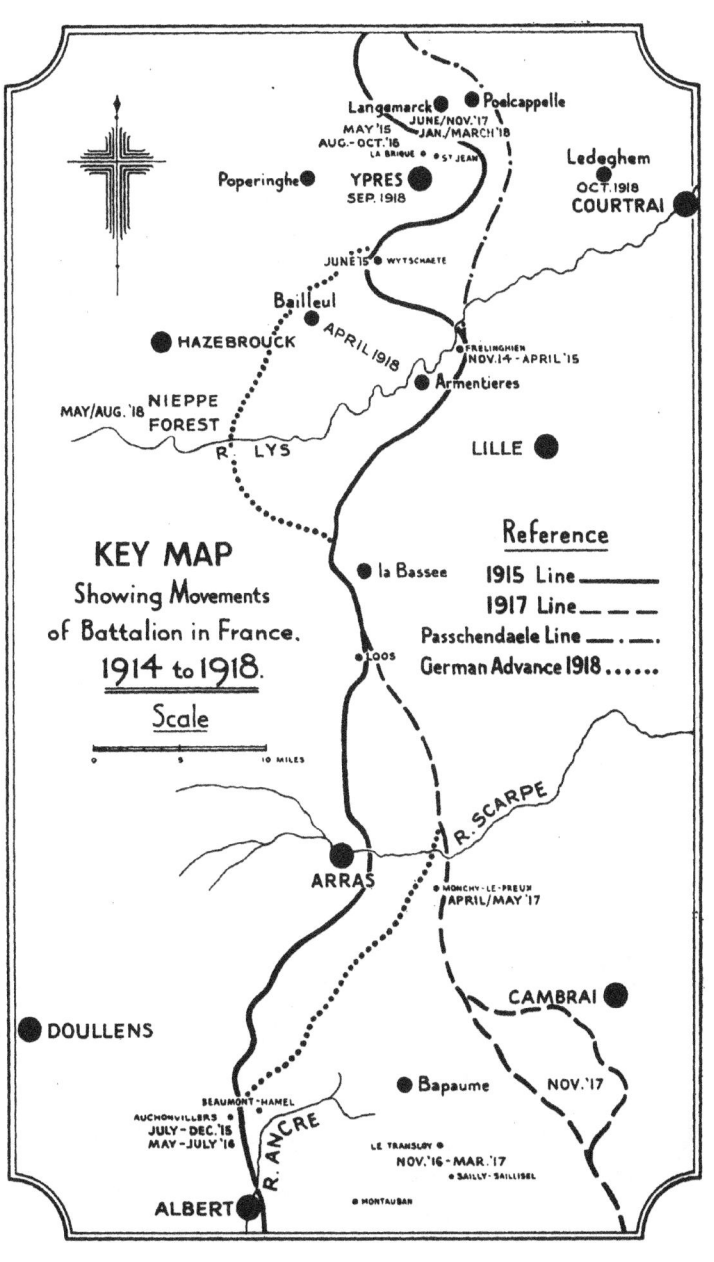

THE COLOURS IN GERMANY.
CORP. W. FOREST.   SERGT. WATKINS.
LIEUT. D. A. ONIONS   LIEUT. L. E. FORD.

Photo by T. S. Winsor.

THE RETURN TO PONTYPOOL.
CAPT. S. ASKEW, M.C.   LIEUT. W. CHARLES.

THE MARCH TO GERMANY

On arrival near the German frontier, the Division rested for a few days, the 2nd Mons. being at Francochamps, where according to the War Diary, attention was concentrated on boots, which had suffered from the long march.

On 4th December the march was resumed and the Battalion crossed the frontier into Germany. No longer were they greeted with cheers, yet the attitude of most Germans towards their conquerors earned their respect. They were usually polite and helpful, always curious to see British soldiers, and obviously glad that the war was over. Cologne was reached on the 9th and the Battalion billeted at Kriel, one of its suburbs. Three days were devoted to " spit and polish," and on the 13th the 2nd Monmouthshires, the only Territorial battalion in Germany, took part in the Triumphal March across the Rhine. All ranks appreciated this to be an historic event, the objective which the Army had striven four years to reach, and each and every man rose to the occasion. The 2nd Mons., therefore, with bayonets fixed, marched proudly through Cologne, past its Corps Commander, over the famous Hohenzollern Bridge and on to Refrath.

On December 20th the Battalion moved to Krahenhohe, in the 9th Divisional area, where two piquets and examining posts were established at river crossings. Here, on the 22nd, the Battalion was drawn up to receive the King's and Regimental Colours which had been fetched from Pontypool by Lieutenants L. E. Ford and H. T. Nelmes, escorted by Sergeant W. Williams, D.C.M., M.M., and Lance-Corporals Dyke, M.M., and Welding.

The Honours List for New Year, 1919, included awards of the D.S.O. to Lieutenant-Colonel Evans, M.C. to Lieutenant H. T. Nelmes, and D.C.M. to C.S.M. Bowen, as well as several M.S.M.'s and mentions in despatches. Those who served under Colonel John Evans will always remember his great pride and confidence in the Battalion, which were justly reflected in the excellent work done for him. He commanded at a time when many of those in France were suffering from the strain of protracted war, but by his cheerful outlook on things in general, and his consideration for all ranks, he maintained the Battalion as a very efficient working and fighting unit.

THE MARCH TO GERMANY

Over ten weeks were spent at Krahenhohe, during which training was carried out and a new subject, education, introduced to the army. Demobilization commenced, resulting in an almost daily decrease in the strength.

On 3rd March the Battalion was relieved and ordered to Dellbrouck for reduction to cadre strength. A large draft of retainable men was transferred to the 9th Cheshires, and a number of others volunteered for service with the Army of Occupation. By the end of the month the Battalion had been reduced to 10 officers and 102 other ranks, who were employed for a time in overhauling stores and packing them for shipment to England. On 19th April further demobilization reduced the cadre to 5 officers and 40 other ranks, and on 27th May they entrained with their wagons and stores for Antwerp, where they embarked on the 31st for Tilbury.

The cadre arrived at Pontypool on 7th June, 1919, to find that a civic welcome had been prepared. The townspeople had gathered *en masse* to do their own battalion honour, and the cadre, on detraining at Crane Street Station from carriages on which they had chalked up " Cologne to Pontypool," " Out in 1914, Home at Last," and so forth, found the streets full of cheering crowds. Colonel Evans and his officers and men were greeted at the station by Mr. A. Densley, chairman of the Pontypool Urban District Council, and escorted in procession to the Town Hall.

After a few days' leave the party proceeded to Prees Heath, near Shrewsbury, where in July the cadre was demobilized and the Battalion disembodied from mobilized service.

On 19th July, a Colour Party consisting of Lieutenant H. T. Nelmes, M.C., Lieutenant H. Ll. Hughes, Sergeant W. Williams, D.C.M., M.M., and Sergeant C. Hayes, D.C.M., representing the Battalion, marched in the Great Peace Demonstration in London.

The Honours awarded by the Battle Nomenclature Committee to the Monmouthshire Regiment for services in the Great War are shown on the title page, those in thick type being carried on the Regimental Colours of all battalions. Of these the 1/2nd Battalion was present at Ypres, 1915, '17 and '18, St. Julien, Frezenberg, Bellewarde, Somme 1916, Arras 1917, Scarpe 1917, Pilckem, Langemarck 1917, Poelcapelle, Cambrai 1917, Lys, Messines 1918, and Courtrai.

CHAPTER IX.

THE 2/2ND BATTALION—THE 3/2ND BATTALION—
THE DEPOT—
1ST VOLUNTEER BATTALION MONMOUTHSHIRE REGIMENT.

THE 2/2ND BATTALION THE MONMOUTHSHIRE REGIMENT.

RECRUITS poured in at the beginning of the War, and as soon as the original battalion was up to strength a second line battalion, the 2/2nd Monmouthshires, was formed under the command of Major J. C. Jenkins. Many of its senior warrant and non-commissioned officers had been drafted from the 1/2nd Battalion, being over the age for active service, and others were men who rejoined the Colours on the declaration of War. In consequence the Battalion was well equipped right in the beginning with efficient instructors.

The Battalion was about 800 strong when in Pontypool in September, 1914. No arms and very few articles of equipment were available, and indeed some time elapsed before all men were in uniform. Training therefore consisted principally of drill, and of route marches to Abercarn, Blaenavon, Cwmbran, etc., all of which helped to stimulate recruiting in these valleys.

When the 1/2nd Battalion went to France the 2/2nd proceeded to Northampton to take their place in the Welsh Division, moving there on 22nd November, 1914. Major J. Evans and details left behind by the 1/2nd had arranged billets for them, and were eventually absorbed in the Battalion. Arms and equipment were issued, and training at once became more advanced than had been previously possible.

In December the Division moved to Cambridge, where the troops were accommodated in college buildings, garages and even boat-houses, while a few more fortunate ones secured

THE 2/2ND BATTALION

billets in private houses. Here the first casualties from overseas battalion joined on being discharged from the hospital.

One of the difficulties of small numbers of men being scattered in billets was the apportionment of rations. It was always some household's turn to have shin-bone of beef, apparently a portion to which landladies were unaccustomed, for they invariably roasted it instead of making it into a stew, much to the disappointment of the hungry soldiery.

Young officers too had their difficulties, due sometimes to unfamiliarity with the drill book. One such cadet managed on a Sunday to get his party to the church successfully but in the excitement of arrival forgot the word necessary to halt the men. Realizing the pressing necessity of stopping, he fell back on the word to which his civilian experience of horses rendered natural to him, and shouted out loudly, " Whoa ! "

During the stay at Cambridge the Division was inspected first by General Sir Ian Hamilton and a few weeks later by HIS MAJESTY THE KING.

In May, 1915, the Division, which later became the 53rd (Welsh) Division, returned to Northampton. It had rather more than its proper complement of battalions, and when in due course it proceeded abroad it took only its first line units with it. The 2/2nd Monmouthshires were thus unfortunately not selected to go overseas, and their service in the War was confined to draft-finding and at first to the necessary duties of the Home Defences. The first draft to the 1/2nd Battalion was despatched as early as December, 1914, and from then onwards the demands were frequent. The Battalion continued also to receive convalescents home from France.

In June, 1915, it moved into Essex, where it was employed for some weeks in constructing trenches in the neighbourhoods of Ongar, Brentwood and Kelvedon for the defence of London from the east. It then returned to Northampton where an opportunity was given to men who had enlisted for home service only to sign for imperial service obligations. Many availed themselves of this, and the remainder went to Cromer where the 2/4th Battalion Monmouthshire Regiment was formed for coastal defence.

THE 2/2ND BATTALION

On 20th July, 1915, the 2/2nd Battalion marched the 26 miles to Bedford, where they took over billets vacated by troops of a Highland division which had gone overseas. Here a lack of fresh vegetables had its effect, and scabies became prevalent. Old members of the Battalion will recall " Scaby Villa " in Shakespeare Road, the Battalion's isolation quarter, and none who experienced them will forget the sulphur baths, or the struggles to get into clothing which had been fumigated : trousers were found to have shrunk to knee length, sleeves to the elbow, soles were burnt off boots, and no shirts or socks were large enough to get into.

In August, 1915, Lieutenant-Colonel Jenkins relinquished the command on appointment to the 1/2nd Battalion, being succeeded by Lieutenant-Colonel Turner after an interval during which Major Charles acted as C.O.

In the spring of 1916 the Battalion moved to Howbary Park, where Lieutenant-Colonel H. J. Miers joined in command. One of the original company commanders of the 1/2nd Battalion in France, he had been invalided home the previous year, and had since then commanded the 5th Suffolks in Gallipoli. He remained in command until April, 1918, when he was appointed to the 2nd East Lancashires in France.

While at Howbary Park, the Battalion provided at short notice 500 men for garrison duties at Sudbourne on the east coast, where Zeppelin raids caused them many excitements and worries. In November the Battalion moved from its camp into winter quarters at Lowestoft and in the following month the Sudbourne contingent rejoined. They remained at Lowestoft until the spring when they went under canvas at Herringfleet, near St. Olaves on the Norfolk Broads. The training of drafts continued without interruption, and men were despatched not to the 1/2nd Battalion only but to all theatres of war and to many units, for the Battalion was by now released from garrison duties and had become purely a draft-training unit.

Returning again to its billets in Lowestoft in the autumn of 1917, the Battalion remained there until the spring of 1918. The system of draft-finding was altered, and men in 1918 were being trained in categories according to their fitness for duty at home or abroad. Gradually, similar battalions of the division had been disappearing, and in April, 1918, the 2/2nd Monmouthshires ceased to exist, its personnel going to France, Egypt, Home Service units and Labour Battalions, in accordance with their medical categories.

Thus ended the 2/2nd Monmouths, a battalion raised originally for home service, which became in the course of time a unit employed solely in training recruits and making them fit in all branches for active service with infantry. Most of the officers of the 1/2nd Battalion did duty at one time or another in the 2/2nd, and a great number of all ranks rested and recuperated in it after wounds and sickness in France.

THE 3/2ND BATTALION MONMOUTHSHIRE REGIMENT.

To deal with recruits and the men of the original Battalion who had returned sick and wounded from France, the 3rd Line, known as the 3rd/2nd Battalion Monmouthshire Regiment was formed in the early days of 1915, and Lieut.-Col. H. D. Griffiths, who retired from the Battalion in 1912 when senior major, rejoined and was appointed to command this new unit. Major Broackes, who had been left in charge of Headquarters, was at first the only other officer.

Colonel Griffiths set to work to find good instructors and he was fortunate in gathering together a number of Warrant Officers who did excellent work in the training and disciplining of the recruits. He motored to Monmouth to look for ex-Sergeant-Major Johnson, who had served with him some years before. They passed each other on the road, Johnson having gone to Pontypool to rejoin. He was made R.S.M. Later, Sergeant-Majors Walker and Letton came from the Depot and were of the greatest assistance in training young Officers and N.C.O.'s. Letton went out to France in 1916 and was killed a few days after his arrival.

During the early days the men were billeted in Pontypool, and Church Halls were placed at their disposal and equipped as Club-rooms, etc. Parades were held in Pontypool Park, and

THE 3/2ND BATTALION

the daily march to the well known strains of " Colonel Bogey " no doubt had a great influence on local recruiting for the Battalion.

An excellent band was formed under Bandmaster S. T. Roderick, and later a beautiful set of silver instruments, costing £400, was purchased with money raised by local residents, these instruments being now the property of the Battalion.

As soon as tents could be provided, a Brigade Camp was formed at Bailey Park, Abergavenny, of the 3rd lines of the 1st, 2nd and 3rd Battalions Monmouthshire Regiment and the Herefords, and Colonel Griffiths was appointed to command.

Equipment arrived slowly but the training of recruits and the reconditioning of the overseas men continued apace, and drafts were constantly being sent to the Battalion in France.

Considerable attention was paid to instruction in trench warfare and the construction of trench and defence works. A system of trenches was dug near the Castle and was elaborately wired. One too spirited charge nearly ended disastrously through the attacking force becoming entangled in these defences.

The Brigade was inspected by General Pitcairn-Campbell and again by General Bethune before the move, in September, 1915, to a hutment Camp at Park Hall, Oswestry, where they remained until March, 1916, when they went into Camp at Whittington. An incident at one of these inspections is remembered. A young officer had cultivated the popular tooth-brush moustache but had reduced this adornment to two minute spots beneath the nostrils. The General paused in front of him, and with withering force said, " Man ! you look like a b——— monkey."

Recruits flowed in steadily and kept up the strength. Indeed, in one fortnight over 900 men joined, an influx sufficient to test the organizing power of any Quarter-Master; but Major Sale, who returned from France just before the move to Abergavenny, was completely unruffled. His work and experience was throughout of the greatest help.

A very fine Canteen, the envy of all other units in camp, was run by some local ladies, and herein the men enjoyed many comforts and privileges. The Tent was presented to the Battalion by Mr. John Paton.

THE 3/2ND BATTALION

The Battalion was always to the fore in games and had a wonderful tug-of-war team which held an unbeaten record. Their success was largely due to the efforts of Sergeant-Major Walker, who coached them daily, but also possibly to the fact that the team were given double rations! Johnny Basham visited the Battalion to give an exhibition of Boxing and was presented with a cigarette case bearing the Regimental Crest.

At this time there were three fully trained Companies of the 2nd Battalion, and there were strong rumours that a Company of the 3rd Mons. was to be added to form a unit to go to France, but requests for more drafts for the 1/2nds prevented this.

Colonel P. G. Pennymore, D.S.O., who was second in command, left to take over the command of a Battalion of Royal Welsh Fusiliers, and Major John Evans took his place. Major H. L. Rosser was also with the unit and Captain H. O. Butler was Adjutant.

The Battalion Musketry record was excellent, thanks to the training received at Prestatyn Musketry School, where Colonel J. C. Jenkins was in command.

In September, 1916, the 3rd Line battalions had been so reduced in numbers by continual drafting to France that it was decided to amalgamate the three Monmouthshire Regiments under the command of Colonel Blethyn Rees (1st Mons.). After a brief sojourn in the old lines at Oswestry this amalgamated Battalion moved to Hutments at Kinmel Park, near Rhyl, where Brigadier-General E. B. Cuthbertson, C.M.G., M.V.O. (late 1/2nd Battalion), was Commandant. In June, 1918, they entrained for Herne, Kent, where they remained in Camp at Strode Park until bad weather in October necessitated removal to Billets in Herne Bay, where they remained until demobilization.

THE DEPOT,
THE 2ND MONMOUTHSHIRE REGIMENT.

A Depot, eventually named No. 234 T.F. Depot, was formed at the Pontypool Drill Hall after the departure of the three battalions, and for the greater part of its existence it was under the command of Major J. G. Broackes. It dealt principally with recruiting and with the posting not only of recruits

THE DEPOT

but of men discharged from hospital. It also acted as a sort of regimental agent, and most non-official articles required by the 1/2nd Battalion were purchased or forwarded through the Depot. In addition, it took charge of non-official documents and records sent home from time to time from France.

1st VOLUNTEER BATTALION MONMOUTHSHIRE REGIMENT.

Early in 1917, the 1st Volunteer Battalion Monmouthshire Regiment was raised for Home Service, and 1,000 Volunteers gave up all spare time to the training. Colonel H. D. Griffiths was in command, with Major Gabb his Adjutant, and a full complement of Volunteer Officers assisted, with a few disabled Officers who had seen service overseas.

A Camp, held at Porthcawl, was attended by 500 men and 53 1st Class Musketry Certificates awarded.

This may perhaps be an appropriate place to record the indebtedness of those who served in the 1/2nd Battalion to many friends for comforts of various kinds sent to them in the endeavour to alleviate the conditions of active service.

The Pontypool Comforts Fund was organized by Mr. Godfrey E. Jones, who acted as treasurer, and Mr. A. C. Fowler. They were generously supported by the Honorary Colonel, Mr. J. C. Hanbury and many ladies and gentlemen of the district, and the Fund supplied a constant stream of sports gear, magazines, socks, shirts, scarves and many other articles, which were deeply appreciated by the recipients. They also sent band instruments at one time.

The *South Wales Argus* sent from its readers large parcels of cigarettes, and the National Fund for Welsh Troops made gifts of footballs and boxing gloves. Among so many friends it is perhaps invidious to single out only the few mentioned above, but the spirit of the times may be envisaged in the gift of a cornet to the Battalion by a London lady who read in the *Daily Express* that the 2nd Mons. were trying to form a band.

CHAPTER X.

2ND BATTALION
THE MONMOUTHSHIRE REGIMENT, T.A.
1920 – 1932.

IN 1920 the auxiliary force was reconstructed and renamed Territorial Army. The re-construction principally affected yeomanry and artillery in the light of lessons learned in the war, and made few changes in infantry organization.

The 2nd Monmouthshires ceased, of course, to be Pioneers and resumed the normal establishment of four companies. Under the county scheme of reconstruction they regained Cwmbran from the 1st Battalion and with the exception of Coleford, which being outside the county was dropped, they retained all their pre-war stations. The Battalion was very quickly up to strength and went to Tenby camp that year full of men who had seen war service.

In 1922, Colonel Sir J. A. Bradney, C.B., T.D., who had commanded for the twenty years from 1892 to 1911, was appointed Honorary Colonel of the Battalion.

On March 3rd, 1923, a memorial to the fallen was unveiled at Trevethin Parish Church by Lieutenant-General Sir Beauvoir de Lisle, K.C.B., K.C.M.G., D.S.O., G.O.C. in C. Western Command, who had commanded the 29th Division during most of the period the 2nd Mons. were in it. The Lord Bishop of Monmouth dedicated the memorial and the Rev. J. W. Hunkin, O.B.E., M.C., sometime Senior Chaplain to the 29th Division, delivered the address.

The Memorial consists of a window and stained glass, a reredos and carved oak tablets on which are inscribed the names of the 539 officers and men who were killed or died in the war. A Book of Remembrance, also containing their names, was placed in an oak desk in the Pontypool Drill Hall.

Colonel W. R. LEWIS, T.D.
Commanding Officer - 1923 - 1933.

2ND MONMOUTHSHIRES, T.A., 1920 – 1932

Lieutenant-Colonel J. Evans, D.S.O., T.D., retired from the command on 20th April, 1923, and was granted the rank of Brevet-Colonel. He had commanded the Battalion for just over six years, including nearly two of Active service.

His successor was Major W. R. Lewis, who had served with the Brecknockshires since 1908 and had seen considerable active service in the Great War, at Aden, in Palestine and in France.

In 1923, in conformity with changes in the regular army, Headquarter Wing was formed to absorb employed men from the fighting companies. As with most Territorial units it was impossible for the 2nd Mons. to establish H.Q. Wing by itself in one or more stations. Consequently, except in camp, when the Wing becomes a separate administrative unit, its personnel and component parts are attached to the nearest of the fighting companies. As far as possible, however, each large group, such as the machine gun platoon, the signal section, the band and drums, was concentrated at one station.

In 1927 the Battalion succeeded in carrying off the Brigade Championship Cup in camp at Porthcawl, and in the following year the Divisional Machine Gun Trophy was captured, together with three of the Brigade Cups.

On the occasion of the PRINCE OF WALES' visit to Cardiff to unveil the National Memorial to Welsh Troops, on 12th June, 1928, the Regimental Band was selected to accompany the Guard of Honour of the 1st Monmouthshire Regiment, mounted at the railway station. At the unveiling ceremony a party, thirty strong, drawn from every detachment of the Battalion, was present under command of Captain G. J. Beard and Lieutenant W. A. C. Matthews.

Machine Gun Companies came into the organization of regular battalions in 1929, and although the corresponding changes in the Territorial Army were not authorized until the following year, the 2nd Monmouthshires adopted the new scheme at once.

As the M.G. Platoon already in existence was at Cwmbran, which was also the headquarters of "A" Company, and as one rifle company had to be converted, the simple plan of making "A" the M.G. Company was accepted. About the same time authority had been received to recruit at Coleford for " D,"

2ND MONMOUTHSHIRES, T.A., 1920 – 1932

the Monmouth company. This enabled Usk to sever its long connection with " D " Company and to become a detachment of the new "A" (M.G.) Company. At the same time the two Pontypool platoons of "A" Company were transferred to the strength of " B " Company.

Since the war the Battalion has resumed the quiet, uneventful tenor of its earlier years, its annual camp being as before the centre around which its life from the personal aspect revolves. Many functions take place during the winter, such as the Officers' and Sergeants' Balls, and the Company Suppers, while the Sergeants' Annual Dinner has become an important feature of Pontypool life.

Courses of instruction are held during the winter months, including many with the regular army. Drills commence in April and now include charabanc trips to selected places for section and platoon exercises. Training in the various weapons on the ranges goes on during June and July, and the Battalion thus gradually works up to the climax of its training, the annual camp.

That the Battalion is endeavouring to emulate its past traditions is shown by one of its members, Private F. J. Cole, who won at Bisley, in 1932, the Gold Medal for the best shot in the Territorial Army.

On Armistice Sunday, each year, the 2nd Monmouthshires march to Trevethin Church and pay their tribute to the memory of those comrades who laid down their lives in the War.

It will be generally regretted within the Battalion that Colonel W. R. Lewis, T.D., who has commanded since 1923 will not be granted a further extension of his tenure of command when it expires in April, 1933. The Battalion has made much progress under his steady and experienced hand and will miss his cheerful leadership when it parts, in the 75th year of its existence, with its seventh C.O.

THE OFFICERS, ABERYSTWYTH CAMP, 1931.

Standing—
The Rev.   Lieut.   Lieut.   Lieut.   Capt.   Lieut.   Sec.-Lieut.   Lieut.
Featherstone   N. de Forth   Hamilton, S.W.B.   R. C. Matthews   N. Honey   T. P. Robertson, S.W.B.   J. G. Woodgates   L. P. Jones   W. A. C. Matthews

Sitting—Capt. J. H. E. Webb   Major D. L. Jones   Colonel W. R. Lewis, T.D.   Capt. G. A. Brett, D.S.O., M.C.   Capt. J. A. N. Beattie

In front—Sec.-Lieut. J. C. Jackson   Sec.-Lieut. T. A. C. Bevan   Lieut. J. F. R. Williams   Lieut. A. T. A. Brown, M.M.

APPENDIX A.

RULES

OF THE

2ND MONMOUTHSHIRE RIFLE VOLUNTEERS,

AGREED TO AND PASSED

At a General Meeting of the Corps, held at Pontypool, on January 5th, 1860.

1.—The Corps having been raised under the Act 44, Geo. III., cap. 54, the Members are consequently subject to the provisions of that Act, and to all regulations which have been or shall be issued, under the authority of the Secretary of State for War.

2.—The Corps shall consist of two classes—(1) ENROLLED Members, consisting of EFFECTIVES, NON-EFFECTIVES, and SUPERNUMERARIES, and (2) HONORARY MEMBERS, the latter contributing to the funds of the Corps, but not being enrolled for service.

3.—The Committee to aid the Commanding Officer in the non-military affairs of the Corps, shall consist of the Commissioned Officers, the Honorary Secretaries, and twelve members of the Corps; which twelve members shall retire at the Annual General Meeting of the Corps, but shall be eligible for re-election. Five to be a quorum; the Senior Officer to preside, and have a casting vote.

4.—All subscriptions shall be paid in advance, and shall fall due on the first day of each year. The Annual Subscription of Commissioned Officers shall be not less than £2 2s. per annum; and of Non-commissioned Officers and Privates, 12s. per annum, to meet the ordinary expenses of the Corps; but such subscription shall not be called up, unless the Committee be satisfied that the funds at the disposal of the Corps render such subscription or any portion thereof, necessary.

5.—The Officer in Command will propose gentlemen to the Lord Lieutenant for commissions, as Officers, but the appointment of all Officers is vested by Act of Parliament in the Lord Lieutenant, subject to the Queen's approval.

APPENDIX A

6.—That the Officers of the Corps, upon appointment, shall pay the following Fees of Honour, exclusive of the fee to the Clerk of the Peace; and on his promotion, the difference between his old and new rank :—

  Captain................... £20
  Lieutenant................ 10
  Ensign.................... 5

7.—That every Non-commissioned Officer shall be appointed by the Officer in command, after consultation with the Members.

8.—Candidates for admission to the Corps must be proposed by two Members, and their names laid before the Committee. The election to be by ballot, at a General Meeting of the Corps. One black ball in five to exclude.

9.—That no candidate for admission be qualified to act as a Member before he has paid his subscription, and given his written adhesion to the rules and regulations of the Corps.

10.—Each Member shall provide himself with Uniform and Accoutrements, which must be in accordance with the sealed patterns selected by the Corps, and approved by the Lord Lieutenant.

11.—Each Member shall be responsible for the due preservation of all articles issued to him, which are the property of Her Majesty's Government, or of the Corps, fair wear and tear only excepted.

12.—The expression " Property of the Corps " shall include all articles which have been purchased out of the general funds, or have been contributed to, or hired by the Corps.

13.—When the Corps is not assembled for actual service, the Commanding Officer is, by the general provisions of the Act 44 Geo. III., cap. 54, solely responsible for the discipline of the Corps; but it shall be lawful for him at any time to assemble a Court of Enquiry, consisting of two Officers and two enrolled Members of the Corps, to be appointed by roster, for the purpose of investigating any irregularity and assisting him in coming to a conclusion upon it; and any Member who shall be proved before such court to have done any act which may injure the harmony or reputation of the Corps shall be liable, at the discretion of the Commanding Officer—who shall consult the Committee before giving his decision—to a fine, a reprimand, or (if not a Commissioned Officer) expulsion; and any Member expelled shall forfeit all interest in the Corps.

  Any inquiry in reference to a Commissioned Officer shall be made by a Court composed of Officers of the Volunteer establishment within the county, convened under the authority of the Lord Lieutenant.

APPENDIX A

14.—The Commanding Officer shall fix the time and place for parades, drills, and rifle practice.

15.—That none but Effective Volunteers, returned as fit for the ranks, be permitted to compete for any prize open to the Members of the Corps. That no Member be allowed to vote at any meeting, or to enter for any prize, until his subscription, and all other sums due to the Corps, have been paid in full.

16.—That the Commissioned Officers shall make such arrangements, subject to the approval of the Commanding Officer, that one, at least, of each Company shall be present at the ordered parade, or whenever a special parade be ordered. In case this rule be broken, each Officer of the Company shall be subject to a fine of 5s., unless it be proved that the non-observance has been occasioned by the neglect of the Officer whose turn it was to be present, in which case that Officer shall be fined 20s.

17.—That the non-commissioned Officers shall make such arrangements, subject to the approval of the Commanding Officer, that at least two Sergeants, and two Corporals, shall be present with the Company as often as it may assemble. In the event of this rule being broken, each non-commissioned Officer of the company shall be subject to a fine of 2s. 6d., unless it be proved which of them is to blame, in which case the offender shall be fined 10s.

18.—Standing Orders are to be exhibited at head-quarters, and the senior Officer in command shall have power, subject to the approval of the Commanding Officer, to inflict fines for disobedience, not exceeding 10s., or less than 2s. 6d.

19.—The following fines shall also be imposed, viz. :—

	s.	d.
For loading contrary to orders, or shooting out of turn	2	6
For discharging the rifle accidentally, or through carelessness	5	0
Drawing swords or bayonets without orders	2	6
For pointing the rifle, loaded or unloaded, at any person without orders	10	0
Talking, laughing, or misbehaving in the ranks	1	0
Being absent from parade at the time of roll-call	0	6
Being absent during the whole time of parade	1	0

These fines to be doubled if it be the Commanding Officer's parade.

Quitting parade without leave of the Superior Officer present	5	0
Coming to parade not properly dressed or accoutred	2	6

20.—All fines imposed on Members of the Corps shall be entered in a book kept by the Commanding Officer for that purpose.

21.—All fines shall become due on the first day of every month succeeding that in which they have been incurred, and shall be collected by the Company's Sergeants, and paid by them to the Commanding Officer, for the general fund.

APPENDIX A

22.—The property of the Corps is, by 50th section of the Act 44 Geo. III., cap. 54, legally vested in the Commanding Officer; but the Committee shall aid him in the management of its finances, and in such other questions as he may refer to them.

23.—The Commanding Officer shall cause an abstract of the accounts to be annually prepared, for the information of every Member of the Corps.

24.—The expense of the ammunition furnished by Her Majesty's Government, as specified in paragraph 21* of the War Office Memorandum of July, 1859, shall be defrayed out of the Funds of the Corps; but the cost of any further ammunition used for purposes of practice shall be defrayed by the Member or Members expending it.

25.—Honorary Members shall severally pay a donation of £5, or an annual subscription of £1.

26.—Honorary Members shall not interfere in any way with the military duties of the Corps, neither shall it be obligatory on them to provide themselves with uniform.

27.—The system of Musketry Instruction, as recommended for Volunteers by the Commandant of the School of Musketry at Hythe, must be adhered to.

28.—Every Member is expected to provide himself with the Rifle Volunteer Manual, and with a copy of the Rules of the Corps.

29.—There shall be a fund raised for giving prizes to the best marksmen in the Corps, under regulations from the Committee, subject to the approval of the Commanding Officer.

30.—That no Member address his Commanding Officer, except through his immediate superior officer.

31.—The Annual Meeting of the Corps shall be held on the first Monday in June. Special Meetings may be convened by the Commanding Officer, at his discretion; but it shall be obligatory on him to summon one, whenever he shall receive a requisition to that effect, signed by twenty-five members of the Corps, and stating the object of the desired meeting. No

* "There will be no special allowance of ammunition for training recruits, but the following uniform annual issues at the cost price, will be sanctioned for the duly qualified effectives, (*See Sections* 5, 6, 7, *and* 8, *of the Volunteer Act*) viz.:—100 Rounds ball per man; 60 ditto blank per man; 176 percussion caps; 20 ditto for snapping practice."

Extract from War Office Circular of Oct. 14, 1859:—

"The amount of ammunition for effective members, to be issued at cost price, on the requisition of the Commanding Officer, is raised from 100 rounds ball per man; 60 ditto blank ditto; 176 percussion caps ditto; 20 ditto for snapping practice—as laid down in the memorandum of 13th July—to 200 rounds ball per man; 120 ditto blank ditto; 352 percussion caps ditto; 40 ditto ditto for snapping practice."

APPENDIX A

business shall be discussed or transacted at any Special Meeting, except that for the discussion or transaction of which the Meeting was convened, unless with the permission of the Commanding Officer. At all Meetings of the Corps, each member shall have one vote.

32.—That all money received for the Corps shall be paid by the Treasurer, without delay, to the credit of the account at the Bank.

33.—That if any case arises not provided for by the preceding Regulations, or if there should be any doubt in the interpretation of them, the Commanding Officer, after consultation with the Committee, shall decide the course to be adopted, and from his decision there shall be no appeal.

APPROVED BY THE SECRETARY OF STATE FOR WAR,

28TH FEBRUARY, 1860.

APPENDIX B

RULES

OF

THE 3RD VOLUNTEER BATTALION SOUTH WALES BORDERERS.

DISCIPLINE.

1. Obedience is the first duty of a soldier, whether regular or volunteer, without it there is no discipline which is the foundation and comfort of a good Regiment.

2. Members when in uniform should at all times be most particular in paying respect to, by saluting, all Officers of their own or other Corps, and of all branches of the service.

3. N.C.O.'s are expected to set a good example in this, and to check any omissions they may observe.

4. Members should at all times bear in mind that when in uniform they have the credit of the Battalion in their hands, which means the reputation of 800 members, and that any unsoldierlike or disgraceful conduct reflects discredit on the whole Battalion; every man should therefore strive to turn out smart, clean, and orderly, in every respect.

5. If a member at any time feels himself aggrieved, he can apply to the Captain of his Company or to the Adjutant, and he will hear the complaint, and if necessary will bring it to the notice of the Commanding Officer.

6. No man is to fall out of the ranks when on the march or parade without the permission of the Officer Commanding the Company.

7. The Officer Commanding can at any time discharge from the Battalion, and strike off the roll any volunteer, for disobedience of orders, or for misconduct, or any sufficient cause.

8. Wearing articles of uniform in conjunction with plain clothes is strictly forbidden, it is both ridiculous and inexcusable, and brings the wearer and his Corps into disrepute.

9. Parcels, bags, or bundles are not to be carried by volunteers when in uniform.

10. Watch-chains, or other articles of jewellery, should not be worn so as to show on the uniform.

APPENDIX B

11. Members must clearly understand it is their duty to at once obey all orders whether received from their own or other Officers or N.C.O.'s, and they should be promptly and cheerfully obeyed in the first instance. If the order is considered an improper one, an appeal may be made through the proper channel, which will always be considered.

RULES.

1. The Commanding Officer is responsible for the discipline of the Battalion, in upholding it he looks for the cordial support and co-operation of all Officers, Non-Commissioned Officers, and Members generally.

In calling their attention to Battalion Rules, he trusts to their good sense and zeal for the proper observance and strict obedience of them, without which he cannot hope to maintain the welfare of the Battalion.

2. These rules to be read to every member before enrolment, each will then be provided with a copy and sign a receipt for the same, thus agreeing to serve under their provisions.

3 The Corps is serving under the Volunteer Act of 1863, and the Members are consequently subject to the provisions of that Act, and of any other Act by which it has been or shall be amended, and to all Regulations issued under the Authority of the Secretary of State for War.

4. The Corps shall consist of two classes:

    (1) Enrolled Members, consisting of Efficients and Non-efficients.
    (2) Honorary Members, who contribute to the Funds of the Corps, but are not enrolled members.

5. Members who do not render themselves efficient in any year, or who are dismissed, shall be required to pay to the funds of the Corps the full amount of the Capitation Grant Proficiency Allowance, or any other Government Allowance at the time in force which they have failed to earn by reason of their non-efficiency or dismissal, and shall return all arms, accoutrements, clothing, and appointments in their possession into store in good order, fair wear and tear excepted.

6. The Commanding Officer shall have power to remit such payment in case of illness or other special reasons.

7. The Commanding Officer will propose gentlemen for Commissions as Officers in accordance with regulations in force for the time being.

APPENDIX B

8. The Non-Commissioned Officers will be appointed by the Commanding Officer.

9. All articles of clothing and all accoutrements shall be in accordance with the pattern approved for the Corps by authority.

10. All accoutrements, and clothing, the property of the Corps, shall be stamped with the initials of the Corps, and with an individual number and date and letter of the Company, before being issued.

11. Each member shall be responsible for the due preservation of all articles issued to him which are the property of the Government or of the Battalion, or any Company thereof, and shall pay for any loss or damage thereto, fair wear and tear excepted.

12. The expression, "Property of the Battalion," shall include all articles which have been or may be purchased out of the General Funds of the Battalion, or have been or may be presented or lent to the Battalion; and the expression, "Property of a Company," shall include all articles which have been or may be presented or lent to any Company of the Battalion, or purchased out of any Private Funds of such Company.

13. Although the Commanding Officer is solely responsible for the discipline of the Corps, he is empowered by Act of Parliament to assemble at any time a Court of Inquiry to enquire into any matter relative to the Corps, excepting the conduct of a Commissioned Officer. Such a Court of Inquiry, when assembled, shall consist of 3 or 5 Members of the Corps, one at least of whom shall be an Officer. Any enquiry in reference to a Commissioned Officer must under Act of Parliament be made by a Court composed of Officers of the Volunteer Forces within the County, convened under due authority.

14. The Commanding Officer shall fix the time and place for parades, drills, and rifle practice.

15. The Senior Officer in Command for the time being of the Corps, or of any Company or Detachment of the Corps, shall have power to inflict the following fines, viz. :

(1) For pointing a rifle loaded or unloaded at any person without orders, 5/-.
(2) For discharging a rifle accidentally or without permission, 5/-.
(3) For having ball cartridge on his person without orders when on parade or drill, 2/6.
(4) For firing at a target when the danger flag is up, or the white disc covering the bullseye, 2/6.
(5) For firing at the wrong target, or shooting out of turn, 2/6.
(6) For aiming or snapping at the target when danger flag is up, 2/6.
(7) For loading before stepping to the front to fire, 5/-.

APPENDIX B

16. All fines imposed on Members of the Corps shall be entered in a book kept under the orders of the Commanding Officer for that purpose, and shall be paid on or before the 1st day of the month succeeding that in which they have been incurred, and shall be collected by the Officer Commanding the Company, and paid to the Commanding Officer who shall place the amount to the credit of the Regimental Funds.

17. The Property of the Corps is by Act of Parliament vested in the Commanding Officer, but a Committee to aid him in the management of the Finances of the Corps shall be appointed annually. It shall consist of the C.O., the Field Officers, and the O.C. Companies, three to form a quorum. The Committee shall meet in May, August, November, and February.

18. The Commanding Officer shall cause an abstract of the accounts to be prepared annually for the information of the members of the Corps, and copies shall be posted at Head Quarters, and the various Drill Halls.

19. Members who desire to leave the Battalion must give to the Commanding Officer 14 days' notice in writing of their intention to do so, they must also deliver up in good order, fair wear and tear excepted, all property whether Government, Regimental, Detachment or otherwise, which may be in their possession as members.

20. No member of the Battalion shall wear his uniform or any part thereof, except for the purpose of Parades or Drills, or at rifle competitions, without obtaining the consent in writing of the Officer Commanding his Company.

21. The members of the Band must not accept any engagement to appear in uniform, or as the Band of the Battalion, without the special sanction of the Commanding Officer through the Band President.

22. None but efficients will be permitted to compete for any prize open to the members of the Corps.

QUALIFICATIONS FOR EFFICIENCY.

Every volunteer in order to become efficient and earn the Capitation Grant must attend a certain number of drills and make a certain score at target practice during each volunteer year, i.e., between the 1st November and the 31st October.

APPENDIX B

The following are the minimum requirements in each case :—

RECRUITS :

1st Year—30 Squad, Company, or Battalion Drills.
60 rounds of ball ammunition in Class Firing, with at least 12 direct hits.

2nd Year—30 Squad, Company, or Battalion Drills, or such number (not less than 9) of Company and Battalion Drills, —3 of which must be Battalion Drills.—as will with the number of drills attended in the first year amount to a total of 60 for two years.

A score of 45 points in the 3rd Class in Class Firing, which must be made in 20 rounds. Three attempts are allowed.

TRAINED VOLUNTEERS.

9 Company and Battalion Drills, 3 of which must be Battalion Drills.
Class Firing. Same requirements as for (*b*).

INSPECTION :

No volunteer must be absent from the Inspection without leave of the Commanding Officer (for which a written application must be made), or unless prevented by sickness, in which case a proper medical Certificate must be obtained.

Any volunteer so absent must attend two Drills IN ADDITION to those above mentioned.

The Rules were passed at a General Meeting held on the Second day of May, 1891.

v.

Approved by Her Majesty Authority 2 Monmouth

o   895

826 *dated Horse Guards,* 20*th day of June,* 1891.

91

APPENDIX C

NOTES ON STATIONS AND COMPANIES.

PONTYPOOL. The fact of the headquarters of two Monmouthshire Volunteer Battalions, both numbered " 2nd " and each with a company in the town, has led not unnaturally to some confusion, which can, however, be cleared up. The raising of a Rifle Corps (later called A Company) by Captain R. B. Roden in 1859, and its expansion into the 2nd Monmouthshire R.V. Corps, has been described in these pages, and Pontypool remained the headquarters of A Company through the several changes of the Battalion's name until the Great War.

The other battalion was the 2nd Administrative Battalion Monmouthshire R.V. Corps (now the 3rd Monmouthshire Regiment), and its Pontypool company, the " Hanbury " Corps, was formed in November, 1859. Under the scheme of reorganization when the Territorial Force was introduced, this company became B Company of the 2nd Monmouthshire Regiment.

After the Great War, in the early days of which the four-company organization was established, the Pontypool detachment remained part of A Company, whose headquarters had moved to Cwmbran. In 1929, when A became the M.G. Company, the Pontypool detachment was transferred to B Company, whose headquarters are at Blaenavon.

The original drill hall at Pontymoile is still used, although now only for storage of certain articles of regimental property, such as tentage, not in frequent use. The present Headquarters Drill Hall in Osborne Road was erected in 1902, the wing now comprising the Officers' Mess and Orderly Room being added after the War.

EBBW VALE. Two Corps were raised in Ebbw Vale in the spring of 1859, becoming Nos. II. and IV. Corps of the 2nd Monmouthshire R.V. Corps. By 1884 they were called C and D Companies, and by 1897 D and E. In 1901 a cyclist company K was raised, but abandoned within two years. On the formation of the Territorial Force the Ebbw Vale detachments went to the 3rd Battalion Monmouthshire Regiment.

APPENDIX C

ABERSYCHAN. The Rifle Corps raised in Abersychan early in 1859 became No. III. of the 2nd Monmouthshire R.V. Corps; in 1884 it was known as C Company and by 1897 it had become G Company. In 1884 H Company was raised at VICTORIA, but no mention of either of these townships appears in the records after 1897. It is probable that the men were absorbed into A or B Companies (Pontypool or Garndiffaith).

SIRHOWY. No. V. Corps of the 2nd Monmouthshire R.V. Corps was raised in Sirhowy in the spring of 1859. By 1884 it had become F Company, a name it retained until it severed its connection of 49 years with the Battalion on being transferred in 1908 to the 3rd Monmouthshire Regiment.

ABERCARN. Abercarn alone shares with Pontypool the distinction of being part of the Battalion in its earliest as well as in the present days, although there was a long gap when the unit was not represented in the township. No. VI. Corps of the original Battalion was raised in Abercarn early in 1859, but the detachment was abandoned probably before 1867. It was revived, however, in 1900, during the recruiting enthusiasm engendered by the Boer War, and became Letter I Company. In 1903 the Ebbw Vale Iron and Coal Company presented a building for use as a drill hall. On the changes due to the inauguration of the Territorial Force the detachment became D Company.

The present fine Drill Hall was built in 1913 and now houses the Drums and one platoon of C Company.

PANTEG. From the earliest days Panteg provided large numbers to the battalion. They probably drilled at Pontymoile, for there is no mention in the records of a drill hall at Panteg until 1884, when the headquarters of G Company were established there. By 1897 this had become C Company, but with headquarters at Upper Pontnewydd, which moved three years later to Cwmbran.

CWMBRAN. Cwmbran was the headquarters of C Company from 1900 to 1908, when the company was transferred through Territorial Force changes to the 1st Battalion Monmouthshire Regiment. In 1920, on the reconstruction of the Territorial Army, Cwmbran was again allotted to the 2nd Battalion, and became the headquarters of A Company (since 1929 A (M.G.) Company).

The present Drill Hall was opened in July, 1925, the miniature range being built in 1930.

APPENDIX C

ABERTILLERY. H Company was raised at Abertillery in 1897, but was transferred to the 3rd Monmouthshire Regiment in 1908.

NEWBRIDGE. The headquarters of E Company were moved from Ebbw Vale to Newbridge in December, 1898, and a strong company was maintained until 1908, when it was absorbed into a new company at Crumlin.

BLAENAVON. A Corps, the 5th, was raised at Blaenavon in October, 1859, becoming a company of the 2nd Administrative Battalion Monmouthshire R.V. Corps, later the 4th V.B., S.W.B. On the formation of the Territorial Force this company came into the 2nd Monmouthshire Regiment, of which it was E Company. After the war Blaenavon became the headquarters of B Company.

The present Drill Hall was built in 1903 and received considerable alterations in 1913. There is an excellent 8-target range a mile from the Hall on the mountain side, where firing at all ranges up to 1000 yards is possible.

MONMOUTH. The 6th Corps, raised at Monmouth in February, 1860, also joined the 2nd Administrative Battalion Monmouthshire R.V. Corps. This company, together with the Usk detachment, became G Company of the 2nd Monmouthshire Regiment in the general changes of 1908.

After the War it became D Company, and in 1928 its headquarters moved from an uncomfortable wooden hut on Chippenham Meads into the east wing of historic Monmouth Castle.

There is an excellent 4-target range at Monmouth.

USK. A company was raised at Usk in May, 1860. It became the 8th Corps and formed part of the 2nd Administrative Battalion. As noted above under Monmouth, it joined the 2nd Monmouthshire Regiment in 1908.

In 1929 it became a M.G. platoon, a detachment of the M.G. Company at Cwmbran.

The range, which for many years had been the practising ground of the many fine shots for which Usk was noted, was surrendered in 1930, on grounds of economy.

LLANHILLETH. A company, F, was raised at Llanhilleth for the 2nd Monmouthshire Regiment at the inauguration of the Territorial Force in 1908. It is now a detachment of C Company.

APPENDIX C

CRUMLIN. In 1892 War Office permission was sought unavailingly to raise a company at Crumlin for the 3rd V.B. S.W.B., but it was not until the Territorial Force changes of 1908 that this town became identified with the Battalion. In that year a company was formed, becoming H of the new 2nd Monmouthshire Regiment.

The present Drill Hall was opened on 24th December, 1910, by Major-General F. Lloyd, C.V.O., C.B., D.S.O., Commanding the Welsh Division, who was accompanied by Mr. J. C. Hanbury, Honorary Colonel of the Battalion. It now houses the headquarters of C Company and the Signal Section.

COLEFORD, GLOS. The Gloucestershire Regiment early had a company at Coleford, but it was abandoned probably because of the remoteness of this portion of the Forest of Dean from their headquarters. In 1912 a detachment of 2 Officers and 85 Men were raised for G Company, 2nd Monmouthshire Regiment, but on the reorganization of the Territorial Army, after the War, Coleford was once more abandoned.

In April, 1930, however, permission was again obtained to recruit for the Battalion in Coleford, and within a month two platoons were formed and posted to D Company. The detachment drills in a hall in the yard of the Angel Hotel.

APPENDIX C

STATIONS OF COMPANIES.

COMPANY.	1861	1877	1884	1897	1901	1908	1927	1930
A	Pontypool	Pontypool	Pontypool	Pontypool	Pontypool	Pontypool	Pontypool and Cwmbran	Cwmbran and Usk
B	Ebbw Vale	Ebbw Vale	Abersychan	Garndiffaith	Garndiffaith	Pontypool	Blaenavon	Pontypool and Blaenavon
C	Abersychan	Abersychan	Ebbw Vale	Upper Pontnewydd	Cwmbran	Garndiffaith	Crumlin, Llanhilleth, Cwmcarn	Crumlin, Llanhilleth and Cwmcarn
D	Ebbw Vale	Ebbw Vale	Ebbw Vale	Ebbw Vale	Ebbw Vale	Abercarn	Monmouth and Usk	Monmouth and Coleford
E	Sirhowy	Sirhowy	Garndiffaith	Ebbw Vale	Newbridge	Blaenavon	—	—
F	Abercarn	Panteg	Sirhowy	Sirhowy	Sirhowy	Llanhilleth	—	—
G	—	Garndiffaith	Panteg	Abersychan	Abersychan	Monmouth and Usk	—	—
H	—	—	Victoria	Abertillery	Abertillery	Crumlin	—	—
I	—	—	—	—	Abercarn	—	—	—
K	—	—	—	—	Ebbw Vale	—	—	—

APPENDIX D.

ROLLS OF OFFICERS.

November, 1861.

LIEUTENANT-COLONEL :
R. B. Roden.

CAPTAINS :
W. B. Hawkins.
W. Adams.
J. Richards.
H. Laxton.
J. B. Hughes.
E. Rogers.

LIEUTENANTS :
— Tothill.
J. Browne.
G. A. Coates.
J. Bladon.

ENSIGNS :
A. Edwards.
T. Mitchell.
P. James.
W. Ratcliffe.

ADJUTANT :
Capt. J. O. Carnegy, 21st F.

SURGEONS :
J. Essex.
E. E. Tucker.

CHAPLAIN :
Rev. W. Hughes, M.A.

September, 1866.

LIEUTENANT-COLONEL :
R. B. Roden.

MAJOR :
J. Richards.

CAPTAINS :
J. B. Hughes.
J. James.
C. Parkes.
T. Mitchell.
P. James.
T. G. Robinson.

LIEUTENANTS :
W. Richards.
R. Jordan.
E. Tucker.
T. L. Skinner.
J. Jacob.

ENSIGNS :
H. Brown.
D. Thomas.
T. G. Bennett.

ADJUTANT :
Capt. J. O. Carnegy, 21st F.

SURGEON :
J. Essex.

CHAPLAIN :
Rev. W. Hughes, M.A.

APPENDIX D

August, 1874.

LIEUTENANT-COLONEL :
R. B. Roden.

MAJOR :
T. Mitchell.

CAPTAINS :
J. S. Cousins.
E. W. Richards.
R. Jordan.
W. H. Powell.
B. M. Mitchell.

LIEUTENANTS :
J. Jacob.
A. J. Strange.
A. L. Davies.
J. J. Richards.
D. M. Llewellin.

SUB.-LIEUTENANTS :
W. H. Davies.
J. N. James.
D. Evans.
R. Jarrett.

ADJUTANT :
Capt. J. O. Carnegy, 21st F.

HON. QUARTER-MASTER :
T. L. Skinner.

SURGEONS :
J. Essex.
J. Davies.

HON. CHAPLAIN :
Rev. W. Hughes, M.A.

July, 1880.

LIEUTENANT-COLONEL :
R. B. Roden.

MAJOR :
T. Mitchell.

CAPTAINS :
W. H. Powell.
B. M. Mitchell.
J. Jacob.
D. M. Llewellin.
A. R. Verity.

LIEUTENANTS :
D. R. Jones.
J. W. Green.

SECOND LIEUTENANTS :
D. L. Evans.
W. A. A. Farr.
J. T. Jenkins.
H. Burnby.
B. Lewis.

ADJUTANT :
Major J. O. Carnegy, 21st F.

QUARTER-MASTER :
H. J. Parkhurst.

SURGEONS :
J. Davies.
J. W. Mulligan.

HON. CHAPLAIN :
Rev. W. Hughes, M.A.

APPENDIX D

October, 1890.

LIEUTENANT-COLONEL :
T. Mitchell (*Hon. Col.*).

MAJORS :
B. M. Mitchell.
J. Jacob (*Hon. Lt.-Col.*).

CAPTAINS :
D.M.Llewellin(*Hon.Major*).
L. N. Wilputte
J. T. Jenkins.
W. O. Dayson.
D. R. Jones.
C. N. Jacob.

LIEUTENANTS :
R. J. Jones.
R. S. Jordan.
J. W. Prosser.
R. Herbert.
A. C. Mitchell.

SECOND LIEUTENANTS :
J. Paton.
R. H. Spencer.
W. E. Phillips.
D. S. Davies.
B. V. Davies.

ADJUTANT :
Major J. O. Carnegy, 21st F.

QUARTER-MASTER :
Capt. H. J. Parkhurst.

SURGEONS :
J. W. Mulligan.
J. R. Essex.
J. W. Davies.

CHAPLAIN :
Rev. J. R. Phillips.

December, 1900.

HONORARY COLONEL :
J. C. Hanbury, Esq., D.L., J.P.

LIEUTENANT-COLONEL :
J. A. Bradney (*Hon. Col.*).

MAJORS :
H. D. Griffiths.
W. E. C. Murphy.

CAPTAINS :
R. H. Spencer.
D. W. Graham.
E. J. Morris.
E. B. Lichtenberg.
W. H. Pitten.
H. Ll. Rosser.
H. Griffiths.
W. Thomas.

LIEUTENANTS :
H. Charles.
J. C. Jenkins.
B. J. Williams.
F. C. Dare.
W. J. Evans.
E. M. Griffiths.

SECOND LIEUTENANTS :
W. A. Lewis.
C. H. C. Mulligan.
A. K. Edmonds.
W. A. James.

ADJUTANT :
Capt. C. G. Beauchamp,
South Wales Borderers.

QUARTER-MASTER :
Capt. A. Sale.

MEDICAL OFFICER :
Surgeon-Major J. R. Essex.

CHAPLAINS :
Rev. D. J. Llewelyn.
Rev. W. E. Williams, M.A.

APPENDIX D

September, 1910.

HONORARY COLONEL :
J. C. Hanbury, Esq., D.L., J.P.

LIEUTENANT-COLONEL :
J. A. Bradney (*Hon. Col.*)

MAJORS :
H. D. Griffiths, T.D.
R. H. Spencer, T.D.

CAPTAINS :
E. J. Morris (*Hon. Major*).
H. Charles.
J. C. Jenkins.
J. Evans.
P.G.Pennymore(*Hon.Major*)
J. G. Broackes.
J. Williams.

LIEUTENANTS :
J. W. Sproule.
A. J. H. Bowen.
E. J. John.
A. H. Edwards.
P. A. Hobbs.
H. W. E. Bailey.
A. J. Bowen.
J. G. Thomas.

SECOND LIEUTENANTS :
E. D. T. Jenkins.
I. E. M. Watkins.
V. H. Watkins.
E. Edwards.
C. H. Moffat.

ADJUTANT :
Capt. G. B. C. Ward,
S. Wales Bord.

QUARTER-MASTER :
Hon. Major A. Sale.

MEDICAL OFFICERS :
Surg. Lt.-Col. J. R. Essex.
Surg. Lieut. E. M. Griffith.

CHAPLAIN :
Rev. E. Morgan, B.A.

Embarkation Roll, 5th Nov., 1914.

LIEUTENANT-COLONEL :
E. B. Cuthbertson, M.V.O.

MAJOR :
C. E. Dansey.

CAPTAINS :
R. A. Hobbs.
A. H. Edwards.
V. H. Watkins
  (Died of Wounds 20-2-15)
A. J. H. Bowen
  (Killed 2-3-17).
J. Ward.
P.G.Pennymore(*Hon.Major*)
E. J. John.
H. J. Miers.
I. E. M. Watkins
  (Killed 5-5-15).

LIEUTENANTS :
J.W.Taylor (Killed 11-3-15).
H. J. Walters (Killed 5-5-15).
P. Hockaday.
L. V. Dart.
A. C. Sale.
A. J. H. Power.
A. E. Frazer (Killed 2-5-15).
J. H. Jacob.

SECOND LIEUTENANTS :
B. A. Williams.
C. Comely.
R. B. Comely.
C. W. Taunton
  (Killed 25-11-16).
J. T. George.
F. L. Newland.
M. G. Perkins.
C. A. H. Hillier
  (Died of Wounds 27-2-15)
J. E. Paton (Killed 31-12-14)

ADJUTANT :
Capt. S. P. A. Rolls, Dorset R.

QUARTER-MASTER :
Hon. Major A. Sale.

MEDICAL OFFICER :
Lieut. G. W. Mason, R.A.M.C.

APPENDIX D

March, 1922.

LIEUTENANT-COLONEL :
J. Evans, D.S.O.

MAJOR :
I. C. Vincent.

CAPTAINS :
C. Cox.
H. H. Watkins.
J. E. Dunn.
E. G. Boucher.

LIEUTENANTS :
D. A. Onions.
T. Gough.
L. A. Mitchell.
G. J. H. Beard.
R. D. Owen.
J. E. T. Matthias.
E. H. Lones.

SECOND LIEUTENANTS :
J. A. N. Beattie.
W. N. Lewis.
D. H. Russell.
R. P. Harris.
C. J. Smith.

ADJUTANT :
Capt. & Bt.-Major C. D. Harris, K.S.L.I.

QUARTER-MASTER :
Capt. G. H. Askew, M.C.

1926.

HONORARY COLONEL :
Col. Sir J. A. Bradney,
C.B., T.D.

LIEUTENANT-COLONEL :
W. R. Lewis, T.D.

MAJOR :
E. G. Boucher.

CAPTAINS :
L. A. Mitchell.
G. J. H. Beard.
R. D. Owen.
J. E. T. Mathias.
T. Gough.

LIEUTENANTS :
J. A. N. Beattie.
W. N. Lewis.
A. B. Jones.
C. J. Smith.
E. A. Johns.
J. H. E. Webb.
W. A. C. Matthews.
J. F. Evans.

SECOND LIEUTENANTS :
D. K. Russell.
H. S. Fish.
R. C. Matthews.

ADJUTANT :
Capt. R. C. Morgan,
South Wales Borderers.

QUARTER-MASTER :
Lieut. N. Honey.

MEDICAL OFFICER :
Capt. J. P. J. Jenkins,
R.A.M.C., T.A.

APPENDIX D

December, 1930.

HONORARY COLONEL:
Col. Sir J. A. Bradney,
C.B., T.D.

LIEUTENANT-COLONEL:
W. R. Lewis, T.D. (*Bt.-Col.*)

MAJORS:
L. A. Mitchell.
D. L. Jones.

CAPTAINS:
T. Gough.
J. A. N. Beattie.
J. H. E. Webb.
J. F. Evans.

LIEUTENANTS:
E. A. Johns.
W. A. C. Matthews.
R. C. Matthews.
J. F. R. Williams.
N. P. N. de R. Forth.
V. G. F. Wickham.

SECOND LIEUTENANTS:
J. G. Woodgates.
A. T. A. Brown, M.M.
T. A. C. Bevan.
J. C. Jackson.
L. P. Jones.
G. A. Hill.
J. Freeguard.

ADJUTANT:
Capt. G. A. Brett, D.S.O., M.C., S. Wales Bord.

QUARTER-MASTER:
Lieut. N. Honey.

MEDICAL OFFICER:
Capt. J. P. J. Jenkins,
R.A.M.C., T.A.

January, 1933.

HONORARY COLONEL:
Col. Sir J. A. Bradney,
C.B., T.D.

LIEUTENANT-COLONEL:
W. R. Lewis, T.D.
bt. col.

MAJORS:
L. A. Mitchell.
D. L. Jones.

CAPTAINS:
J. A. N. Beattie.
bt. maj.
J. H. E. Webb.
W. A. C. Matthews.
J. F. R. Williams.

LIEUTENANTS:
R. C. Matthews.
N. P. N. de R. Forth.
V. G. F. Wickham.
J. G. Woodgates.
A. T. A. Brown, M.M.
T. A. C. Bevan.

SECOND LIEUTENANTS:
L. P. Jones.
G. A. Hill.
J. Freeguard.
E. P. Lewis.
K. D. Treasure.

ADJUTANT:
Capt. J. S. Windsor, M.C., South Wales Borderers.

QUARTER-MASTER:
Capt. N. Honey.

MEDICAL OFFICER:
Capt. J. P. J. Jenkins,
R.A.M.C., T.A.

APPENDIX E

HONORARY COLONELS.

J. C. Hanbury, Esq., D.L., J.P.	1892 – 1921
Col. Sir J. A. Bradney, C.B., T.D.	1922 –

COMMANDING OFFICERS.

Colonel R. B. Roden	1858 – 1887
Colonel T. Mitchell	1887 – 1891
Colonel J. A. Bradney	1892 – 1911
Lt.-Col. E. B. Cuthbertson	1911 – 1915
Lt.-Col. A. J. H. Bowen, D.S.O.	1915 – 1917
Colonel J. Evans, D.S.O., T.D.	1917 – 1923
Colonel W. R. Lewis, T.D.	1923 – 1933

ADJUTANTS.

Major J. O. Carnegy, 21st Foot	1861 – 1891
Captain J. H. Travers, S. Wales Bord.	1891 – 1896
Captain C. G. Beauchamp, ,,	1896 – 1901
Captain H. A. Moore, ,,	1901 – 1904
Captain L. H. Thornton, Rifle Brigade	1904 – 1906
Captain G. B. C. Ward, S. Wales Bord.	1907 – 1912
Captain S. P. A. Rolls, Dorset Regt.	1912 – 1915
Captain A. C. Sale, 2nd Mon. Regt.	1915
Captain M. F. Turner, M.C. ,,	1915
Captain T. L. Ibbs, M.C. ,,	1915 – 1918
Captain R. T. Saunders ,,	1918 – 1919
Major C. D. Harris, K.S.L.I.	1920 – 1923
Captain C. H. Morgan, S. Wales Bord.	1923 – 1927
Captain G. A. Brett, D.S.O., M.C. ,,	1927 – 1931
Captain J. S. Windsor, M.C. ,,	1931 –

APPENDIX F

CAMPS.

2ND MONMOUTHSHIRE RIFLE VOLUNTEER CORPS
- 1880 and 1881 Llanthewy Skerrid.
- 1882 and 1883 Newport Barracks.
- 1884 Raglan.

3RD V.B. S.W.B.
- 1885 Llancayo.
- 1886 Abergavenny.
- 1887 Aldershot.
- 1888 Brecon.
- 1889 Ewenny.
- 1890 Minehead.
- 1891 Ewenny.
- 1892 St. Arvans.
- 1893 Woodbury, Nr. Exmouth.
- 1894 Porthcawl.
- 1895 and 1896 Tenby.
- 1897 Aldershot.
- 1898 Brecon.
- 1899 Porthcawl.
- 1900 Bulford (Salisbury Plain).
- 1901 and 1902 Porthcawl.
- 1903 Towyn.
- 1904 Parkhouse (Salisbury Plain).
- 1905 Minehead.
- 1906 Conway.
- 1907 Porthcawl.

2ND BN. MON. R. (T.F.)
- 1908 Porthcawl.
- 1909 Ammanford.
- 1910 Bow Street.
- 1911 Lamphey.
- 1912 Hereford.
- 1913 Porthcawl.

2ND BN. MON. R. (T.A.)
- 1920 and 1921 Tenby.
- 1922 Aberystwyth.
- 1923 and 1924 Porthcawl.
- 1925 Isle of Man.
- 1926 and 1927 Porthcawl.
- 1928 Cheltenham.
- 1929 Porthcawl.
- 1930 Holyhead.
- 1931 Aberystwyth.

APPENDIX G

HONOURS AND AWARDS
EARNED IN THE
GREAT WAR, 1914-1918.

The Battalion was mentioned in despatches three times for meritorious and efficient services.

C.M.G.

Lt.-Col. E. B. Cuthbertson, M.V.O.

D.S.O. AND BAR.

Lt.-Col. A. J. H. Bowen.

D.S.O.

Lt.-Col. J. Evans.
Lt.-Col. H. J. Miers.
Capt. (Hon. Major) P. G. Pennymore.

M.C. AND BAR.

Major T. L. Ibbs. Captain R. B. Comely.

M.C.

Sec. Lieut. C. E. Birkett.
Capt. C. Comely.
Sec. Lieut. H. B. Davies.
Major A. H. Edwards.
Capt. J. T. George.
Lieut. H. J. Hopkins.

Capt. W. D. Howick.
Lieut. H. T. Nelmes.
R.S.M. J. Noble.
Lieut. & Q.M. W. M. Porter.
Sec. Lieut. W. R. Sankey.
Capt. M. F. Turner.

APPENDIX G.

CROIX DE GUERRE (FRENCH).

Sgt. J. Counsell.
Capt. A. L. T. Robertson.
Capt. R. T. Saunders.

Dmr. D. White, D.C.M.
Sgt. W. Williams, D.C.M., M.M. (265363).

CROIX DE GUERRE (BELGIAN).

Capt. R. B. Comely, M.C.
Cpl. W. Rose.

Sgt. A. Watkins.
Cpl. G. Whitfield.

ORDER OF ST. STANISLAUS.

Lt.-Col. E. B. Cuthbertson, C.M.G., M.V.O.

CROSS OF ST. GEORGE.

Sgt. T. Yates, D.C.M.

MENTIONS IN DESPATCHES.

Capt. H. W. E. Bailey.
Lt.-Col. A. J. H. Bowen, D.S.O. (three times).
Lieut. W. T. Charles.
L/Cpl. W. H. Chick.
Sgt. F. Collins.
Capt. R. B. Comely, M.C.
Sgt. J. Counsell.
L/Sgt. H. C. Cox.
Lt.-Col. E. B. Cuthbertson, C.M.G., M.V.O.
Sec. Lieut. J. E. Dunn.
Major A. H. Edwards, M.C.
Cpl. R. Emery.
Lt.-Col. J. Evans, D.S.O. (twice.)
Lieut. A. E. Fraser.
L/Sgt. A. Hodges.
Lieut. H. J. Hopkins, M.C.
Sec. Lieut. H. L. Hughes.
Major T. L. Ibbs, M.C.
Lieut. H. V. Kerr.
Sgt. H. E. Mason.

C.S.M. G. S. Mellsopp.
Lt.-Col. H. J. Miers, D.S.O. (twice).
R.S.M. J. Noble, M.C.
Lieut. R. M. Nott.
Sgt. D. O'Leary.
Lieut. I. E. Owen.
Sec. Lieut. J. E. Paton.
L/Cpl. G. Rappel.
R.Q.M.S. C. E. Richards.
Pte. J. H. Robinson.
Lieut. R. T. Saunders.
Capt. F. L. Spencer.
Capt. M. F. Turner, M.C.
Cpl. S. Vaughan.
Sgt. E. Wagstaffe, M.M.
Lieut. H. J. Walters.
C.S.M. T. E. White.
C.S.M. C. Williams.
Sgt. G. Wilson.
C.S.M. G. T. Yearsley, D.C.M.

APPENDIX G

D.C.M.

R.S.M. W. J. Bowen.
L/Sgt. J. Dowding.
Cpl. T. A. Drew.
Pte. H. Hemmings.
Pte. W. G. Hemmings.
C.S.M. J. Johnson.
Pte. G. Jones.
Pte. J. Lewis.
C.S.M. C. Love.
Pte. J. Mogford.

Pte. J. Morgan.
Sgt. A. E. Pinchin.
Sgt. J. Roberts.
Sgt. W. Spiers.
Dmr. D. White.
Sgt. W. Williams (265363).
Sgt. W. Williams (265503).
Sgt. G. Yates.
Sgt. T. Yates.
R.S.M. G. T. Yearsley.

M.M. AND BAR.

Sgt. A. J. Cross.

Sgt. J. McNichol.

M.M.

Pte. E. Andrews.
Cpl. J. J. Bayes.
Sgt. R. S. Beddin.
L/Cpl. G. Bedford.
Cpl. A. Belli.
Pte. S. J. Burnett.
Pte. W. Burnett.
Sgt. D. Dallimore.
L/Cpl. A. Dyke.
Pte. D. Evans.
Pte. T. Greenslade.
Sgt. C. Griffiths.
Pte. J. Griffiths.
Sgt. J. Hale.
L/Cpl. H. Hatherall.
Sgt. W. Jenkins.
Sgt. J. Jones.
L/Sgt. W. Jones.

Pte. J. Lewis.
Sgt. C. H. Lock.
L/Cpl. J. Phillips.
L/Cpl. R. J. Pole.
Cpl. S. Powell.
L/Cpl. M. R. Price.
C.Q.M.S. C. Pritchard.
L/Cpl. T. Rose.
Pte. L. Schofield.
Sgt. A. E. Smith.
Cpl. R. Trew.
Sgt. A. Turner.
Sgt. E. Wagstaffe.
L/Cpl. F. E. Williams.
L/Cpl. J. J. Williams.
Sgt. W. Williams, D.C.M. (265363).
Pte. E. Wilson.
Pte. T. Withey.
L/Cpl. W. Woodland.

M.S.M.

Sgt. R. A. Booth.
Sgt. R. Evans.
Cpl. C. H. Grey.
Sgt. C. Hayes.
Sgt. Hopkins.

C.Q.M.S. G. E. Phillips.
Sgt. E. J. Pikes.
Sgt. T. Priddle.
Sgt. A. E. Smith.
C.Q.M.S. F. Wall.

ROLL OF HONOUR

OF THOSE MEMBERS OF THE
1/2ND BATTALION THE MONMOUTHSHIRE REGIMENT
WHO LAID DOWN THEIR LIVES IN THE
GREAT WAR, 1914-1918.

OFFICERS.
LIEUT.-COL. BOWEN, A. J. H., D.S.O. AND BAR.

CAPT.	LIEUT.	2ND-LIEUT.
EDWARDS, E.	SANKEY, W. M., M.C.	DAVIES, E. O.
HOCKADAY, S. R.	SPENCER, F. L.	FRAZER, A. E.
WATKINS, I. E. M.	TAUNTON, C. W.	HILLIER, C. A. H.
WATKINS, V. H.	TAYLOR, J. W.	JONES, F. T. A.
	WALTERS, H. J.	KING, A.
LIEUT.	WILLIAMS, J. R.	LAWLOR, E. F.
FRASER, J. H.		PATON, J. E.
OWEN, I. E.	2ND-LIEUT.	REED, H. W. T.
PERCIVAL, R. F.	COLLINS, W., M.C.	TAYLOR, F. H.
ROSENBAUM, L. S.	CRUICKSHANK, R.	WILLIAMS, W. J.

COMPANY SERGEANT-MAJORS.

BOOTH, W. J.	DOWSE, H.	GRANGER, J. S.

COMPANY QUARTER-MASTER-SERGEANTS.

ALLSOPP, W. J.	BOWEN, H. T.

SERGEANTS.

BEDDIN, R. S.	EDWARDS, W.	PERRY, A. E.
BERROW, G.	HOPKINS, W. G.	POWELL, R. J. (M.M.)
BUTCHER, J.	JACKSON, J. (M.M.)	PROSSER, W.
BUTCHER, T. J.	JENNINGS, F. G.	RODEN, S. J.
CHAMP, J.	JONES, J.	RUCK, S. R.
COLLINS, F.	KILMINSTER, H. W.	SMART, S.
COOKE, W. T.	KNIPE, G. E.	WEST, J.
DAVIES, A.	MEADMORE, G. M.	
EDWARDS, W.	PARSONS, W.	

ROLL OF HONOUR

LANCE-SERGEANTS.

LLYWARCH, J. ROBERTS, W. TREW, R. E. (M.M.)

CORPORALS.

BIRT, H. G.
COX, S.
CRABB, W.
CUDBY, J.
DURBIN, W.
EVANS, T.
FLETCHER, P. L.
FLETCHER, P. L.
HARRHY, E.
KENNEDY, M.
LEWIS, R. K.
MCCARTHY, E.
MORRIS, W. D.
PARSONS, G.
REES, H. C. S.
RICHARDS, W. J.
SKILLMAN, F.
SLADE, G. H.
TOTTERDELL, L. W. C.
VAUGHAN, S.
WILLIAMS, C.
YARWORTH, R.

LANCE-CORPORALS.

ACKROYD, R.
BEVAN, J.
BIRKIN, A.
BOWEN, T.
BRIMBLE, H.
BUTLER, V.
CAREY, W.
DAVIES, C. G.
DAVIES, P.
EDWARDS, C.
EVANS, E.
HAVARD, E.
HOLMES, H.
HORTON, A.
JARRETT, G. M.
JENKINS, A.
JONES, C.
JONES, H. B.
JONES, H. C.
JONES, P.
JONES, W.
KEEFE, W.
LEWIS, H.
LEWIS, J.
LEYSHON, W. J.
LONG, E.
LOVELL, G.
MULLARNEY, E.
PAYNE, J.
PAYNE, T.
PEARCE, A.
PRITCHARD, J.
ROBERTS, G. T.
ROBERTS, T. H.
SHORT, A.
SYKES, F. G.
THOMAS, D. H.
THOMAS, W. H.
TURNER, I.
UNDERWOOD, G.
WEBLEY, W. H.
WHEATLEY, E.
WHEATLEY, G.
WILLIAMS, C.
WILLIAMS, F.
WOODFIELD, G.

PRIVATES AND DRUMMERS.

AINSWORTH, A.
ARCHER, P.
ARTHUR, W. A.
BADGER, J. C.
BADHAM, G. C.
BAGGS, A. C.
BAKER, F. S.
BALL, A.
BALSOM, F.
BATSTONE, H.
BAYNTON, T.
BEBBINGTON, C.
BELL, J.
BENNETT, W. W.
BEVAN, W. G.
BIBEY, J.
BIGGS, T.
BLACKWELL, S. H.
BLANCHARD, S.
BLEWITT, F.
BOND, C. H.
BOWEN, W.
BRADFORD, A.
BRIDLE, P. W.
BROOKS, G. F.
BROTHERTON, J.
BROWN, A.

ROLL OF HONOUR

PRIVATES AND DRUMMERS.

BROWN, C. A. H.
BROWN, T.
BROWN, W. J.
BRYANT, G. C.
BULLOCK, A. J.
BURNETT, J. G.
BURNS, S.
BUTCHER, W.
BUTLER, F.
BUTTERWORTH, W.
CAINES, F.
CARMAN, T. P.
CARPENTER, G.
CAWSEY, W. H.
CHANCE, W. G.
CHANEY, J. H.
CHISNALL, W.
CHIVERS, G. F.
CHIVERS, J.
CIANTAR, A.
CLANCY, R.
CLANCEY, M.
CLARKE, A. R.
CLARKE, E.
CLARKE, J.
COLE, R. H.
COLE, R.
COLEMAN, T.
COMPTON, H.
CONIBEAR, E. E.
CONNOR, J.
COOK, G. W.
COOK, R. G. H.
COOPER, E.
COOPER, G.
COOPER, J.
CORBETT, C. A.
CORKE, J. E.
COX, G. L.
CROWLEY, W.
DACEY, D.
DARBY, H.
DARE, H. W.
DANIEL, R.
DAVIES, A. G.

DAVIES, D.
DAVIES, D. L.
DAVIES, F.
DAVIES, G.
DAVIES, G. T.
DAVIES, G. A.
DAVIES, J. J.
DAVIES, J. H.
DAVIES, J. P.
DAVIES, L.
DAVIES, L. J.
DAVIES, S. G.
DAVIES, W. E.
DAY, A.
DAY, J.
DIX, A.
DORAN, E.
DOWNES, A. H.
DOWNEY, W.
DRAPER, D.
DRUMMOND, T. E.
DUKES, A. E.
EACUPS, F. W.
EASTOP, C. H.
EDWARDS, H.
EDWARDS, J.
ELSON, J. E.
EMMOTT, F.
EVANS, E.
EVANS, F.
EVANS, F.
EVANS, H. H.
EVANS, J.
EVANS, J.
EVANS, J. H.
EVANS, J. T.
EVANS, S.
EVANS, T. C.
FLEETWOOD, A.
FLYNN, D.
FOLEY, J.
FORD, W.
FRANCIS, J.
FROST, A. E. W.
GALLIVAN, T.

GAUGHAN, P.
GARNETT, J.
GEORGE, L.
GEORGE, W.
GIBBS, A.
GIBSON, E.
GOODALL, E. J.
GOUGH, E.
GOULDER, C.
GRAHAM, G.
GRANT, F. E.
GREEN, R. W.
GREGSON, J.
GRIBBLE, W.
GRIFFITHS, A.
GRIFFITHS, C.
GRIFFITHS, D. G.
GROVES, A.
GUEST, H.
GUNN, A.
GWYN, T. H.
HAINES, J. W.
HALL, H.
HAM, F. C.
HAND, H.
HARDACRE, J.
HARDINGE, E. W.
HARRINGTON, D. J.
HARRIS, A.
HARRIS, J. A.
HARVEY, A.
HAVARD, T. B.
HARWORTH, H.
HAYMONDS, T. J.
HAYWOOD, N.
HERRINGTON, F. R.
HICKS, J. P.
HIGGS, W.
HILLIER, F.
HITCHINGS, W. H.
HOLBEY, S.
HOLDEN, T.
HOLMES, F.
HOLMES, M. W.
HOLLAND, W.

PRIVATES AND DRUMMERS.

HOLLINSHEAD, W.
HOLVEY, S.
HOUGH, J. P.
HOWELLS, W.
HUNT, A.
HUGHES, F.
JAMES, A.
JAMES, B.
JAMES, J. M.
JAMES, J.
JAYNE, J.
JENKINS, A.
JENKINS, E. F.
JENKINS, J.
JENKINS, P.
JENKINS, S.
JOHN, E. G.
JOHNS, J.
JOHNS, W.
JOHNS, W. P.
JOHNSON, H. R.
JONES, A. J.
JONES, A.
JONES, F.
JONES, F.
JONES, G.
JONES, H. L.
JONES, J.
JONES, L.
JONES, R.
JONES, R.
JONES, S. H.
JONES, T. J.
JONES, W. E.
JONES, W. H.
JUKES, T.
KELLY, J. J.
KENNEDY, T.
KENYON, H.
KING, W.
KINGS, H. G.
KIRTLAND, C.
KYNASTON, D.
LAMPARD, C.
LANE, W. J.

LANGLEY, J.
LAWTON, A.
LEDDINGTON, W. G.
LEINTHALL, W.
LESTER, G. T.
LEWIS, F.
LEWIS, G.
LEWIS, J.
LEWIS, J.
LEWIS, N.
LEYSHON, W.
LILWALL, A. E.
LINDLEY, H.
LINNEY, C.
LITTLER, J.
LLEWELLYN, W. J.
LLOYD, R.
LLOYD, W.
LONG, E.
LOWE, A.
McLAREN, D.
MAGNESS, T.
MARSDEN, H.
MARTIN, T.
MATHER, H.
MATTHEWS, E. W.
McLOUGHLIN, T.
MEADMORE, E. W.
MERCER, A.
MEREDITH, D.
MEREDITH, T. G.
MERRY, G.
MICHAEL, H.
MIDDLE, H. H. J.
MILLS, C. J.
MITCHELL, E.
MOGFORD, J.
MORGAN, J. A.
MORGAN, F. W.
MORGAN, J. L.
MORGAN, S.
MORGAN, T.
MORGAN, W. H.
MORRIS, F.
MORRIS, T.

MORRIS, T. E.
MORSON, W. J.
MORT, H.
MOSLEY, H.
MURPHY, W.
MURRAY, C.
MURRAY, J.
MURRAY, T. H.
NEEDS, W.
NEWMAN, R. T.
NEWMAN, W.
NICHOLLS, F. P.
NICHOLLS, W.
NICHOLAS, J. S.
NUNNERLEY, A.
NURDIN, A. S.
OATES, D.
ORMESHER, A.
OSBORNE, J.
OWEN, G. T.
PADFIELD, J.
PALFREY, E.
PARFITT, J. H.
PARKER, J.
PARRY, T.
PARRY, W.
PATTIMORE, S.
PAUL, A. E.
PAUL, R.
PAYNE, C.
PAYNE, H. W.
PHILLIPS, E.
PHILLIPS, J. H.
PHILLIPS, S.
PHILPIN, J.
PHIPPS, W.
PICKFORD, J.
PIERCE, E. F.
POINER, C. T.
PORTER, W.
POWELL, C.
POWELL, D.
POWELL, G.
PREECE, A.
PREECE, E. C.

PRIVATES AND DRUMMERS.

PREECE, E.
PRESTON, C.
PRICE, A.
PRICE, B.
PRICE, D. R.
PRICE, J. L.
PROSSER, T. J.
PUGH, D.
PYE, J.
RALPHS, T.
REES, R. W.
REES, R. W.
REES, T.
REYNOLDS, D. J.
RICHARDS, D. J.
ROBERTS, A.
ROBERTS, C. J.
ROBERTS, D. J.
ROBERTS, E.
ROBERTS, G.
ROBERTS, H. P.
ROBERTS, J.
ROBERTS, R. C.
ROGERS, J.
ROGERS, S. T.
ROWBERRY, E. C.
ROWLAND, A.
ROWLANDS, T.
SAGE, W. J.
SAUNDERS, J. H.
SAUNDERS, T. G.
SAVORY, H. L.
SAVERY, R.
SCANNELL, P. J.
SCHOLES, G.
SHAW, H.
SHAW, J.
SHEA, J.
SHEEN, J. S.

SHERRATT, E.
SMITH, E.
SMITH, G.
SMITH, H.
SMITH, J.
SMITH, S.
SMITH, T.
SOUTHERN, R.
STEPHENS, A.
STEVENS, G. T.
STIFF, C. W.
STONE, W. J.
STRONG, T.
STROUD, W. J.
STURKEY, R.
SYMONS, F. J.
TARLING, T. J.
TAYLOR, A.
TAYLOR, H.
TAYLOR, R. J.
TEAGUE, W. T. E.
THOMAS, C.
THOMAS, E.
THOMAS, E.
THOMAS, J. G.
THOMAS, T. J.
THOMPSON, W.
TINDALL, G.
TUNLEY, W. J.
VAUGHAN, A.
VAUGHAN, T. H.
VERNALL, C.
VERNALL, J.
VEYSEY, J. A.
WALKER, A.
WATKINS, H.
WATTS, J.
WATTS, W.
WARBRICK, G. R.

WARREN, W. J.
WAYGOOD, G.
WEAVER, H. P.
WEEKS, P.
WELSH, W.
WHITCOMBE, W. J.
WHITE, B.
WHITE, C.
WHITE, G.
WHITE, T.
WHITTAKER, A.
WHITTINGTON, H. H.
WHITTLE, C.
WILLIAMS, A.
WILLIAMS, A. W.
WILLIAMS, A. V.
WILLIAMS, C.
WILLIAMS, C.
WILLIAMS, E. D.
WILLIAMS, H.
WILLIAMS, H.
WILLIAMS, H.
WILLIAMS, L.
WILLIAMS, R.
WILLIAMS, R.
WILLIAMS, R.
WILLIAMS, S.
WILLIAMS, W.
WILLEY, G.
WILSON, C. R. (M.M.)
WINWOOD, H. V.
WITHERS, J.
WOODS, H.
WOODS, W.
WYATT, H. G.
YOUNG, G.
YATES, F.

www.ingramcontent.com/pod-product-compliance
Lightning Source LLC
Chambersburg PA
CBHW031146160426
43193CB00008B/267